I0752489

The MAN FROM VERMONT

The MAN FROM VERMONT

CHARLES ROSS TAGGART
THE OLD COUNTRY FIDDLER

· Adam R. Boyce ·

Published by The History Press
Charleston, SC 29403
www.historypress.net

Front cover: Charles Ross Taggart as "The Old Country Fiddler," circa 1900. *Courtesy of the Newbury, Vermont Historical Society.*

First published 2013

ISBN 978.1.5402.2234.3

Library of Congress CIP data applied for.

Notice: The information in this book is true and complete to the best of our knowledge. It is offered without guarantee on the part of the author or The History Press. The author and The History Press disclaim all liability in connection with the use of this book.

To Charles Ross Taggart, known by multitudes of grateful audiences as "The Man from Vermont" and "The Old Country Fiddler" (1871–1953)

To my loving wife, Mary-Anne Boyce, without whose help in so many areas this book wouldn't have been possible

CONTENTS

FOREWORD

I was named after my maternal grandfather, Charles Ross Taggart. He and his wife, Edna, lived with us from pretty soon after I was born, over seven decades ago now, until I was in my mid-teens. His primary years as an entertainer were behind him by the time I began to understand who he was, beyond just "Grandpa." He was the tall, white-haired man who constantly practiced the fiddle in his room and who often told stories at the dinner table.

Sooner or later, some of those stories got to be familiar enough that I knew what they were about and what was funny about them. The same was true of songs, like "The Cat Came Back," and poems like "The Raven," both of which ended in sepulchral tones that could give me the shudders. And he did teach me tricks of drawing that helped me much in developing my artistic avocations as time passed.

He took me with him on walks in Pisgah National Forest in western North Carolina—we lived at the edge of the woods—where he would dig out sassafras roots for tea. When my father was transferred to southern Arizona by the Fish and Wildlife Service, Grandpa and I once climbed to the flat top of a mesa in the San Carlos Apache reservation, and we looked out across the rugged southwestern landscape, dotted with saguaro cacti. A couple years later, after we'd moved to College Station, Texas, he unsuccessfully tried to interest me in learning something about music. I was too much of an adolescent then to understand what an opportunity that was—or to understand that his time with us was limited.

FOREWORD

My father retired due to health reasons, and my Grandma's health was failing—she passed away there in Texas in 1950. From that point, my Grandpa's life, too, began to fail. We moved to New England to give him a chance to see his old haunts, including the house, Elmbank, in Newbury, Vermont, where my mother and his other two daughters had grown up. They looked up many friends who were still around. All of this was new stuff to me, of course, though the place names and people were familiar from family reminiscences. Grandpa died soon afterward in Maine.

Adam Boyce's book, as well as his living history portrayal of "The Old Country Fiddler," provides you with a wonderful view of my grandfather's life and work, a view that I welcomed because it helped me know much better a man and an artist about whom I frankly had not had a chance—nor had I taken the opportunity—to become better acquainted with when he was alive. For this, I will always be immensely grateful.

ROSS CHAMBERLAIN
grandson of Charles Ross Taggart
Las Vegas, Nevada

PREFACE

I first heard about Charles Ross Taggart through an Internet search for "old time fiddling," sometime just after 2001. I listened to some of his "Old Country Fiddler" records online, and at first, I wasn't very impressed. This was probably due mainly to the less-than-ideal sound quality but also the subtleness of the humor.

Later, I inherited several volumes of *The Vermonter* magazine, a collection that had belonged to my aunt and uncle, noted historians Miriam and Wesley Herwig of Randolph Center, Vermont. In this collection, which spanned the late 1890s through 1945, I found a copy from late 1927 that had an interesting photo on the front cover. It showed a fiddler, dressed in a suit, wearing a felt hat, cupping his right ear and leaning toward a floor-model phonograph with a delighted expression on his face. It was a poke at the Victor Records advertising icon, the Victor dog, Nipper, who could "Hear His Master's Voice," and it was also advertising the fact that Charles Ross Taggart had put out recordings of his humorous monologues—thus the subtitle: The Old Country Fiddler Hears his Own Voice.

It was also humorous to see a large headline directly below the photo, which had nothing to do with Taggart. Just a short time before the publication of this issue, the Great Flood of 1927 had occurred, which literally devastated Vermont. Besides the cover photo of Charles Ross Taggart and the interview with him inside (with two more photos of Taggart), this volume of the magazine had several photos and stories relating to the disastrous flood, and so the large headline under Taggart's photo read:

Preface

Going Thro Hell and High Water

Talk about placement!

In a roundabout way, this unrelated flood headline seems to fit with the life of Charles Ross Taggart. It is an amazing story, filled with ups and downs, and plenty of "high water," both literally and figuratively. The more I found out about him, the more interesting he became—a man who spent his life traveling around the country, making a living by doing what he enjoyed: entertaining others with his various talents. How could he be anything *but* interesting!

I had started giving lectures to nonprofit groups in 2002 through the Vermont Humanities Council, and in 2006, I started doing the same thing in New Hampshire. I thought Mr. Taggart would make an interesting subject. However, I went on to other things, and "The Man from Vermont" was put on the back burner for awhile.

Then, in 2009, I started in earnest to find more information about Charles Ross Taggart, with hopes of bringing him to twenty-first-century audiences—not as a lecture, but as a living history portrayal. Since I played the fiddle, and I was able to get some digital copies of some of his recordings, I thought I would be able to put together a reasonable representation of him. Remarkably, I had an old felt hat (originally a woman's hat, I believe) that I had found upstairs in my grandfather's corn barn many years earlier. For some reason, I had saved it, using it for various theatrical productions over the years. It was perfect for Mr. Taggart's "Old Country Fiddler" outfit!

In his later years, writing from College Station, Texas, circa 1946, Mr. Taggart sent an article about his life and career as a traveling musical humorist to what was a new magazine, namely *Vermont Life*. Unfortunately, the magazine never published the article. I came across a copy of this unpublished article in the archives of the Newbury (Vermont) Historical Society in 2010 and thought that I would try to interest *Vermont Life* in finally recognizing Mr. Taggart. Once again, Charles Ross Taggart's life story was rejected by them. However, *Vermont Magazine*, a different publication, ran a very fine article about both of us in its November/December issue of 2011. It intertwined our respective life stories, as well as my efforts at bringing him back to life (so to speak). It was an honor to have Mr. Taggart's story included with my own.

Since being added in 2010 to the humanities program lineups in both New Hampshire and Vermont, "The Old Country Fiddler" has been very well received. Once again, he is in the limelight and is being given the attention and recognition he richly deserves.

Preface

In putting together the living history portrayal of Taggart, I found that I had acquired a huge amount of information about him that just couldn't be included in a single live presentation. There were bits and pieces about Charles Ross Taggart from many different sources and locations. A biography was needed to consolidate these items, and this is my attempt at doing so. Having said that, I'm sure there are more things waiting to be discovered about Taggart, as he traveled so extensively throughout North America.

It is hoped that you will enjoy following the life and journeys of "Charlie" Taggart and that you will develop your own personal connection with this remarkable piece of our cultural past.

Adam R. Boyce
West Windsor, Vermont
June 3, 2013

ACKNOWLEDGEMENTS

Grateful acknowledgement is due the following for their kind assistance in this project:

Pat Stark, Newbury (Vermont) Historical Society

Doris McClintock, Newbury, Vermont

Newbury (Vermont) Town Clerk's Office

Bill Hodge, Topsham (Vermont) Historical Society

Topsham Town Clerk's Office

Evelyn Potter, Readfield (Maine) Historical Society

Kathryn Hodson, Special Collections Department Manager, University of Iowa Libraries at Iowa City

Peter Weis, Northfield Mount Hermon School, Northfield, Massachusetts

Ross Chamberlain, grandson of Charles Ross Taggart, Las Vegas, Nevada

Dayle Dooley, archivist, Congressional Cemetery, Washington, D.C.

Acknowledgements

Clarence Davis, Public Records Administrator and Historian, District of Columbia

Nanci Young, archivist, Smith College, Northampton, Massachusetts

Emerson College, Boston, Massachusetts

New England Conservatory of Music, Boston, Massachusetts

Katharine Blaisdell, North Haverhill, New Hampshire

Mary-Anne Boyce, my wonderful wife, for her untiring efforts in creating the index

A special thanks to the following Vermont publications for allowing reprinting of letters and articles, or portions thereof, written by or about Charles Ross Taggart:

Bradford Journal Opinion (former *United Opinion*)
Barre-Montpelier Times Argus (former *Barre Daily Times*)

Chapter 1

IN THE BEGINNING

East Topsham, Vermont, has changed little in the course of the past 140-some odd years. True, technology and transportation are quite a bit different now, as well as social and political viewpoints. However, East Topsham was—and still remains—an isolated community of indomitable people. This was the place that was home to a talented young man, a future entertainer, searching for his place in the world and searching for ways to share his numerous skills, as well as earn a living—a young man who would travel far and wide across North America, far from the remote location of East Topsham, bringing joy and wonderment to thousands of people with music, stories, ventriloquism and various tricks.

The name Charles Ross Taggart is still known in the town of Topsham, which consists of three hamlets: West Topsham, Waits River and East Topsham. His name is also familiar in the towns of Newbury and Bradford. Old record collectors know his "Old Country Fiddler" recordings very well. Beyond that, his name and cultural contributions are virtually unknown or unremembered, as few—if any—people are still alive who remember seeing Taggart perform in person. Yet his story is a true American success. Granted, he might not have been rich or famous, but he was able to make his way doing the things he truly enjoyed. There was a price for this success. Taggart endured many long periods of time and distance away from family and friends, making him lonely. He enjoyed few comforts on the road. Full meals and stationary beds were luxuries that he rarely had. Travel itself could prove dangerous at times, and it was miraculous that Taggart made it to most of his destinations. Of course, once in awhile, he missed a connecting train, as trains didn't always arrive on time, due to various situations. Taggart would then have to resort to other means of transport, including early automobiles, horses or even "Shank's Mare," i.e., walking. On these occasions, he often arrived late, finding the appointed venue locked up and dark. There was nothing he could do about it except proceed to his next engagement. Such was the life of a traveling entertainer.

"The Man from Vermont" was born in Washington, D.C., on March 19, 1871. His mother, Emily (Divoll) Taggart, was born and raised in East Topsham, Vermont, in the house that her grandfather, Asa Divoll, built in the late 1790s. It was a large farm, consisting of 150 acres, south of East Topsham village, high on a hill. Emily's father, Josiah Divoll, was a farmer, like his father before him, and a devoutly religious man. Emily's mother, Lucina (Peabody) Divoll, died when Emily was only seven. Josiah Divoll was, at one time, an elder in the Scotch Covenator Church in the village, part of the New Reformed Presbyterians. Emily was brought up in this church and apparently felt so strongly about her faith that she became a missionary, leaving East Topsham and going to Washington, D.C., about 1865 to work at a Freedmans' mission there.

We don't know the particulars of how she met her husband, John Nelson Taggart. John Taggart was presumably from Pennsylvania and had served in the Union army during the Civil War. We don't know exactly where in Pennsylvania he was from or anything about his military service. We do know that John and Emily met in Washington. They were married there in 1866, and John worked for a time as a postal clerk in Washington.

The Taggarts had two children prior to Charles's birth—a girl and a boy. The girl,

A photo of Charlie Taggart's mother, Emily (Divoll) Taggart, taken in Washington, D.C., circa 1865. *Courtesy of the Topsham, Vermont Historical Society.*

The East Topsham, Vermont home that Charlie Taggart first knew, which was originally built by his great-grandfather, Asa Divoll, in the late 1790s. Charlie lived here from the time he was two until about six years of age in 1877, when his grandfather, Josiah Divoll, sold the 150-acre farm on the hill for a smaller one in East Topsham village. Photo is circa 1900, and individuals shown are believed to be the J.R. McLam family. *Courtesy of the Topsham, Vermont Historical Society.*

Mary Evelyn Taggart, born in 1867, lived about a year and a half, while the boy, John Divoll Taggart, born in 1869, died less than one year after his birth. By October 1870, John and Emily were expecting another child to come in the spring of 1871. John Taggart became ill and died unexpectedly on October 27, 1870, at the age of thirty. On the very same day of his death, his grave site was purchased, and he was buried in the Congressional Cemetery in Washington, D.C. Emily Taggart, now a widow and expecting a child, was alone. When her son, Charles, was born five months later, Emily, still in Washington, managed to collect a widow's pension for her late husband's war service.

When Charles was about two years old, he and his mother, Emily, relocated to the place she had originally called home: East Topsham, Vermont, at her father's farm. This is the spot where "Charlie" Taggart was introduced to the Green Mountain State and the community he would call home for the next thirty-four years. Around 1877, Charlie's grandfather, Josiah Divoll, sold his 150-acre farm, purchasing a home just south of the gristmill in East Topsham village, eventually buying a small farm—about 30 acres—diagonally across the road from the church and the town hall. Emily Taggart acquired a small home for Charlie and herself, a little bit west of the center of East Topsham village and a short distance from her father.

Josiah Divoll farm in East Topsham village, where Charlie Taggart lived for some time in the 1890s. *Courtesy of Mary-Anne Boyce.*

Emily apparently had the wherewithal to have not only her own house but also a melodeon—a reed-type pump organ. The new home was close to the village schoolhouse, where Charlie attended. However, the widowed mother understood that art and culture were just as important as reading, writing and arithmetic, and she tried to expose her young son to as many "good" things as she could, including fine literature and music.

Around the time Charlie was seven or eight, Emily took him by horse and buggy seven miles to Groton to hear a musical company—the Baker Family. The experience was not lost on young Charlie, who reminisced many years later that he could still remember Mr. Baker, the patriarch of the troupe, playing the violin and plucking the strings on the tune "Grandfather's Clock," imitating the ticking of a clock. As soon as they got home, young Charlie set about building his own violin out of wood and wire, even borrowing some tail hair from their mare to build a bow for his creation. The "instrument" Charlie built wasn't exactly musical, but the experience prompted his mother to explore his interest in music. Emily Taggart arranged for a Swiss-born itinerant music teacher named John Erhl to come to their home and give young Charlie music lessons—first on their melodeon, and then later, it is believed, on the piano. Erhl gave music lessons to several pupils throughout the area, traveling by horse and buggy.

Emily decided that young Charlie needed more professional instruction than Mr. Erhl could deliver and made arrangements for her son to take piano lessons in Montpelier. Charlie recounted this many years later in an interview with Lois Goodwin Greer, which appeared in the *Vermonter* magazine in November 1927: "I used to drive...seven miles, twice a week, to Groton, where I left the old horse in a friend's barn, then went by train to Montpelier for piano lessons. I returned on the late afternoon train, harnessed up the horse and drove back over the hills to Topsham. Did this twice a week for a long time, either with a horse or bicycle."

In the late 1940s, Charles Ross Taggart wrote an article about his life and career, which he sent to the newly created *Vermont Life* magazine. The article, for whatever reasons, was never published. Fortunately, a copy of the rejected article still exists in the archives of the Newbury, Vermont Historical Society. In this article, Taggart writes that he played the fife in the East Topsham village Drum Corps and later "led a band and played for a County Fair," probably in Bradford, which consisted of members from the Topsham and East Corinth area. Taggart played several instruments during his lifetime, including the piano, cornet, trumpet, violin, fife, banjo and slide trombone.

Charlie Taggart, in the 1927 *Vermonter* interview, related his leaving East Topsham in 1889 to attend the Mount Hermon School in Northfield, Massachusetts, saying, "Mother finally sent me to Mount Hermon to school...In my class at Mount Hermon were the now famous magician, Howard Thurston, and Lee DeForest, who made the radio a practical thing by the invention of the Audion tube."

Emily Taggart, on Charlie's application to enter Mount Hermon, noted how good Charlie was, stating, "I don't think he lives in the indulgence of any bad habit," and that "he is aiming to live a devoted Christian life." His health was listed as "good," and to the question of peculiarities, she wrote, "nothing worthy of mention," although she added, "He has a peculiarly sensitive temperament, but has a good deal of self-control. Mirthfulness, as well as [conscientiousness], is marked in his character. He has quite a musical talent."

In answering the question, "Why do you wish to send him to this school," Emily wrote, "As his character is not fully formed, I wish him to be in a good school, safe from the temptations to which he might be more exposed in other schools...that he may have the healthful exercise that your school holds out—although in good health, he has never been able to endure too much confinement to study."

Emily listed on the application that young Charlie had taken "common English...Latin and Algebra" and had "given some attention to Physics, Physiology and Physical Science." She also noted that Charlie especially liked Latin "and has given a little attention to German (without a teacher)." Emily added that Charlie "has never been fully able to decide on an occupation."

Charlie's minister, the Reverend J.C.K. Faris, was listed as a reference, and Reverend Faris wrote of Charlie, "I can commend him as a worthy young man, conscientious, having no bad habits, and of very good natural abilities."

Another reference, the Topsham Town Clerk, J.R. McLam, wrote that Charlie "is a boy of good moral character and good habits, and a good [scholar] for one of his age. One of our best boys, and of a good family."

Although Charlie was in the class of 1893, taking the "Scientific Course," he was barely able to finish the first year due to homesickness, frail health and possible financial considerations. The following letter, which he wrote to his mother, Emily, detailed some of his thoughts while at Mount Hermon:

Jan. 16th, 1890

My Dearest Mother,

I received your letter last night, also the pills and box of candy and thoroughwort. How good you were to think of them. I think the candy helped to loosen my cough and the thoroughwort gave me an appetite...I have not been out doors since Sat. night, but I get up every day and make my bed and keep on my clothes through the day, although I lie in bed.

I eat a little, to keep my strength up, for I am very weak. They bring me over my meals.

I never appreciated home any more in my life than these days.

I feel as though I don't know what is best for me to take and there is no one except you and the nurse to ask, and she stays down to the hospital... however, I have not been very lonesome, for I have read a good deal in the Youth's Companions and Golden Legacy, etc.

I keep your picture on the mantle piece [where] *I can see it, and it seems as though you were looking upon me, and I feel better.*

Why Mamma, I have thought since I have been sick that it would be just paradise to be at home and working on the farm helping Grandfather and having good, robust health: doing good and earning money. I believe that farming is, as you have always said, what we shall have to go into after I leave school. There was nothing in it that I ever disliked, except the hard work, and I don't think that I shall ever be very healthy without plenty of outdoor exercise. I was a fool to ever think that old Topsham was the worst place that I could be in. It's the only home I ever knew, and I have found that I have a great deal of love of home and country, which I didn't know I had so much [of] *before. I believe I could be happy and contented (if I had my health) to come home and work on the farm, and you could keep boarders, and wouldn't we be happy.*

> *Perhaps we can, after I leave school. Well, I have been letting my thoughts run just about as they came, and you know how to take them...*
>
> *Your letter comforted me much. Please write immediately—again, if you have time...But I must say Goodnight.*
>
> *Your loving Charles*

Charlie came home from Mount Hermon in the summer of 1890. On August 30 of that year, Charlie wrote from Topsham to the superintendent of Mount Hermon, informing him that he wouldn't be able to come until Thanksgiving or Christmas vacation "as I have taken a school to keep," i.e., teaching at a local one-room school. He seems to have kept putting off returning to Mount Hermon, according to subsequent letters he wrote to the school, and it is doubtful he ever *did* return as a scholar, although Mount Hermon officially noted that Charlie "left" on December 19, 1891.

He *would* return to Mount Hermon, in later years—not as a scholar, but as a traveling entertainer. Charlie gave several benefit performances for the school over the years, as well as financial donations. Throughout the remainder of his life, he always found time to write a few lines to his would-be alma mater.

Upon his return to Vermont from Mount Hermon, Charlie found employment in Bradford as a clerk in Osbourne's General Store and at the local express office. After the death of his Grandfather Divoll on April 13, 1891, Charlie resigned his Bradford positions and came home to help his mother run his grandfather's farm there in East Topsham village. Thus began a jack-of-all-trades career for the twenty-year-old Charlie, which he spoke of in his interview with the *Vermonter*:

> *And along with my farming enterprise—and I had four cows and quite a bit of land—I taught music all over the country-side, going from house to house as had my former teacher and predecessor, John Erhl, with a horse and buggy; and during the school year I taught the "deestrict school," and in the evening the singing school. But with my farming a little, teaching day school, singing school and piano a little, and tinkering watches a little, I was not progressing very rapidly either in a professional or business way. It wasn't particularly profitable.*

By some means, Taggart was able to attend two institutions in Boston, Massachusetts, in late 1894 and early 1895: the Emerson School of Oratory (now Emerson College) and the New England Conservatory of Music, where he studied voice and piano. He never graduated from either school, spending about a semester at each. The weekly Bradford, Vermont newspaper, the *United Opinion*, related the following Topsham news:

March 15, 1895
The East Corinth & Topsham Coronet Band will be heard from later on, with C.R. Taggart, who has recently returned from Boston where he has been studying music, as leader.

July 12, 1895
C.R. Taggart has purchased a colt and a fine top buggy.

In the 1927 interview with the *Vermonter*, Charlie Taggart admitted, during this time period, to being "very unsettled in my mind, and considered it highly desirable to do something a good deal—not a little."

A life-changing direction for Charlie came later in 1895, when he happened to be at the Topsham Post Office. He saw a poster there advertising an "entertainment" to be given in Groton by a Mr. Frank G. Reynolds of Boston. Charlie and his mother decided to attend, traveling by horse and buggy. It was a memorable performance, as he reminisced in the *Vermonter:*

> [Mother and I] *were both very much delighted and pleased, not only with his program, but with the man himself, and quite upon my own initiative, I asked Mr. Reynolds to go to* [East] *Topsham to give one of his entertainments. Of course, Mother entertained him at our house when he came to* [East] *Topsham, and I confided to him the inspiration which had been born in me during his program at Groton. No man could have been more attentive and interested* [in helping me] *than he was. He told me all about his own work, how he arranged his programs, went over every little detail, and finally advised me to try myself out* [in public].

Charlie Taggart had quite a few talents and reasoned that he *should* be able to put together some sort of debut program of music and recitations of "pieces" he had learned, including some ventriloquism, which he had picked up while at Mount Hermon "with some difficulty." Friends and family thought he was simply going through a phase in his life and that the idea of entertaining would leave him. Quite the contrary: it only got bigger in his mind. However, the prospect of performing in public was a bit intimidating, and while Charlie had worked up a program of thirteen numbers in his mind, incorporating cornet, violin and banjo, he kept putting his debut off, until one day, according to Charlie, in the *Vermonter* interview:

> *While I was driving to West Topsham* [to give piano lessons]*...I thought I would try out, by myself, some of my Conservatory and Emerson*

> *things...but it "kinder" scared me to think of it. As I approached the turn of the road, I thought I'd leave it to the old horse to make the decision. If he turned at the foot of the hill, I would go on and hire the village hall and leave an order at the printer's for my* [hand]*bills and tickets; on the other hand, if the horse turned up the hill where I was going to give the piano lessons, the die would be cast. When we got to the bottom of the hill, I "kinder" pulled the rein a little mite, and we went on and hired that hall.*

The date of Charlie's debut was October 8, 1895, at the Topsham Town Hall in East Topsham village. According to a publicity sheet of Taggart's, circa 1910, he came to the hall that night "dressed in his Sunday clothes, with his cornet, banjo and fiddle under his [buggy] seat; while the expectant villagers waited with baited breath for the treat that was in store for them." He continued his recollections in the *Vermonter* magazine article:

> *I had a good crowd. Came out of curiosity. The night of the performance, I drove to the village, hitched my horse under the meeting-house sheds, then I*

Charlie Taggart was a master of trick photography. Here he appears in one of his own photos as two different individuals—himself, in his normal traveling attire on the right, and as an old farmer on the left. It is believed that this is the front of the Topsham Town Hall in East Topsham village, where Charlie debuted as an entertainer on October 8, 1895. Photo is circa 1905. *Courtesy of the Newbury, Vermont Historical Society.*

> *climbed the stairs to the hall, lit the lamps, placed a small table by the door, distributed my change, and waited. Admission was fifteen cents, children ten. When the hall was fairly filled, I asked a friend to take my place at the door, and then I proceeded to the stage to give my entertainment.*

Charlie Taggart had started his performance that night with a cornet solo, and his circa 1910 publicity sheet stated, "Altho' quivering with excitement, he blew forth the opening blasts with a grand flourish. He forgot nothing, and as he warmed to his work, and felt the magnetic thrill of sympathy with his audience, he was intensely happy; and his face was flushed with a glow of excitement and joy as the people came to congratulate him at the close."

In his interview in the *Vermonter*, Charlie went on with the details of that evening:

> *I drove home that night with my heart filled with exultation, and my pocket filled with change. After I had put up my horse, I spread out my earnings of the evening—nine dollars and fifty cents—and when I had deducted a dollar for the hall, and another for the printing, I had the grand total of seven dollars and a half. That was the first money my talents ever earned me, but I have kept them busy with more or less success ever since.*

Taggart's circa 1910 publicity sheet goes on to say, "He reasoned thusly: If this can be done once, it can be done again, and it was, and has been done under varying conditions ever since."

Charles Ross Taggart had embarked on what would become his life's work: entertaining as a musical humorist to countless audiences all over the North American continent. For a time following his first public performance, he practiced and honed his craft fervently by entertaining solely in his own area of East Topsham and surrounding communities. Charlie shared his talents locally, in schools and churches, under a profit-sharing plan. However, the reality was that long-term success and financial security would not be possible simply by doing these performances exclusively within his locale. Charlie would have to branch out to other areas, leaving the one place he knew and loved the most. He was about to open the door to a completely different world and a completely different way of life than he knew in East Topsham.

Chapter 2

MOVING UP

We don't know very much about Edna Elizabeth Little, Charlie Taggart's wife. She was born in Bremen, Maine, on October 18, 1871, to Thomas and Sarah (Morse) Little. Edna attended Smith College in Northampton, Massachusetts, which wasn't too far away from the Mount Hermon School in Northfield. It doesn't appear that she and Charlie Taggart knew each other at that time because Edna had started at Smith in 1891, well after Charlie had left Mount Hermon. She is listed as being a member of the class of 1895, but she, like Charlie, never completed her education. For unknown reasons, Edna left in 1894, halfway through her third year of school. She had been working toward obtaining a bachelor of arts degree. By 1896, Edna was a resident of Washington, D.C.

We also don't know exactly how Edna and Charlie met, but obviously, they did, and they liked each other—very much. We do know that they were married on March 3, 1896, at 921 P Street in Washington, D.C., by the Reverend F.D. Power of the Vermont Avenue Christian Church. It is presumed that 921 P Street was Edna's residence at the time. Charlie brought his bride home to East Topsham to begin their lives together on the village farm owned by his late Grandfather Divoll.

Charlie and Edna were expectant parents in February 1897. Edna gave birth to twins—one was their first daughter, Evelyn; the other, a stillborn. In May 1899, another daughter was born—Miriam, known in the family as Bonnie. A son was born on October 13, 1900, but died in infancy. Daughter

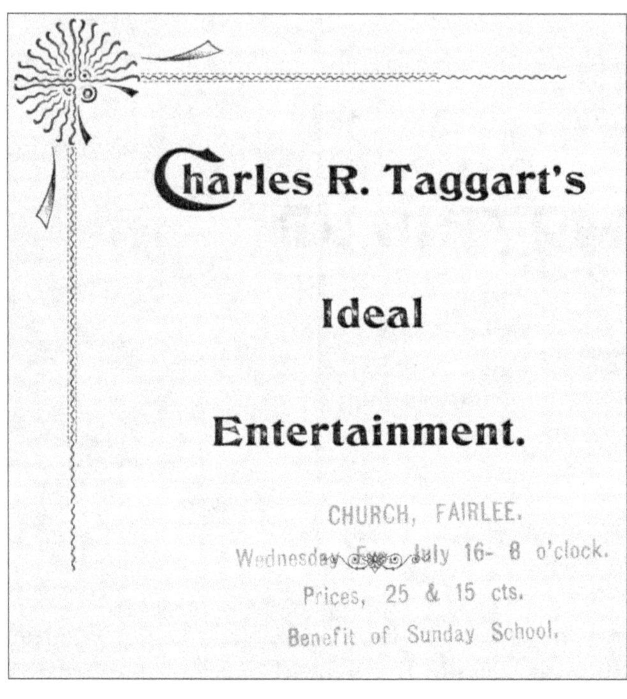

Charles R. Taggart's

Ideal

Entertainment.

CHURCH, FAIRLEE.

Wednesday Eve, July 16- 8 o'clock.

Prices, 25 & 15 cts.

Benefit of Sunday School.

This page and opposite: Front and insides of an early Charles Ross Taggart program, circa 1900. *Courtesy of the Newbury, Vermont Historical Society.*

Specimen Program.

PART I.

Songs.

The Old Guard,	*Rodney*
Nearing the Harbour,	*Davis*
Bill the Bosun,	*Jude*

Readings.

Scene from Julius Cæsar,	*Shakespeare*
Our Guides,	*Mark Twain*

Piano Selections.

Spinnerlied,	*Mendelssohn*
Romanza Impassionata,	*John Orth*

Dialect Readings.

Address to a Louse,	(Scotch)	*Burns*
Sockery Setting a Hen,	(German)	

Ventriloquial Dialogues.

PART II.

Songs.

a Die Beiden Grenadiere, *Schuumann*

b Off for Philadelphia, *Haynes*

c Negro Melodies, Banjo Accompaniment

Impersonations.

Character Sketches from David Copperfield, *Dickens*

a Mr. Micawber.

b Uriah Heep.

c Mr. Peggotty.

Piano Selections.

a Tarantenella, *Heller*

b Frisches Leben, *Spindler*

c Chacone, *Durand*

Song.

Selected.

What they say.

Charles R. Taggart gave a most unique and pleasing entertainment at the Passumpsic Baptist Church last evening. For one man to give an entertainment of an hour and a half as vocalist, musician, reader and impersonator, and hold his audience breathless with admiration is a wonderful thing. His rendering of Poe's "Raven" exceeded in expression and pathos anything I had ever heard.

Mrs. S. Louise Barton, Evangelist and Lecturer, Boston, Mass.

Last evening, in the M. E. Church, Charles R. Taggart gave a very acceptable entertainment consisting of readings, impersonations and vocal and instrumental music. The interest of the audience was not allowed to flag for even a moment. The people will eagerly look forward to the next annual visit of Mr. Taggart.

Irving C. Brown, Pastor M. E. Church.

Monroe, N. H., Aug. 27, 1897.

Mr. Taggart has several times entertained Ryegate audiences—his latest appearance here being the present season, when before the Christian Endeavor Society and their friends he rendered a very acceptable program. As he alone can easily fill out an evening with a varied and interesting program we would most heartily recommend Mr. Taggart to all C. E. Societies wishing to give an enjoyable high-grade entertainment.

Edith B. Gibson, Pres. Y. P. S. C. E.

Ryegate, Vt., Dec. 6, 1898.

Mr. Charles R. Taggart's entertainments are of superior merit. His selections, both musical and literary, display excellent taste and good judgment. Either as vocalist, instrumentalist, or dramatic reader, he never fails to capture his audience. His impersonations are masterpieces and well deserve the hearty applause which they receive.

Sam'l A. Jackson, Pastor, Reformed Presbyterian Church.

So. Ryegate, Vt., Feb. 2, 1899.

Elisabeth, nicknamed "Abou" (pronounced ah-BOO), was the last of the Taggart children, born March 17, 1907.

With a wife and family to support, Charlie had more reasons than ever to make his entertaining career successful. Frank G. Reynolds, the traveling one-man entertainer from Boston who inspired and mentored Charlie, came to visit the Taggarts annually at their East Topsham home. During one of these visits, Reynolds suggested that Charlie get into the Boston Lyceum Bureau and helped him to do so.

While part of the Boston Lyceum Bureau, Charlie Taggart was discovered by the head of a local entertainment bureau there in Boston. In the *Vermonter* magazine interview in 1927, he recalled the experience:

> *One time, I was in Cambridge, Mass., and unknown to me, Mr.* [A. Abbott] *Lovett, of the Lovett Entertainment Bureau in Boston, dropped into the auditorium. After* [my] *performance, he came to me and told me to come into his office some day, and he would see what he could do for me. The thing he "did for me" was to send me down to the Butler Insane Hospital in Providence* [Rhode Island]. *I suppose he thought if I made a hit there, he would try me upon a sane audience. He was evidently satisfied with the result of the experiment because he immediately became my manager.*

Taggart's early programs emphasized classical music and the recitation of fine literature, but with the passage of time, he saw that humorous stories, impersonations and mimicry, accompanied by music, were more enjoyable to people of all ages and backgrounds. His "pianologues" were mostly humor with fine music, but "The Old Soldier's Vision" was a favorite patriotic number. He added numerous alter egos to his routines, which he called "character sketches," changing into different costumes right before the eyes of his audience. Charlie performed ventriloquism, throwing his voice to make it sound as if a little boy was hiding in the nearby upright piano. He referred to this "little boy" as his "ventriloqual assistant." He also created a number of original stories and characters, including his famous "Pineville Folks" monologues, based loosely on real people from back home in the East Topsham area. Although he primarily used his own material, Charlie occasionally borrowed from leading humorists of the day, including Mark Twain, Will Carleton, Bill Nye and Artemus Ward. He was also known for a burlesque rendition of Edgar Allan Poe's "The Raven."

The Lovett Entertainment Bureau gave Charles Ross Taggart the moniker that would stay with him for the rest of his career: "The Man from

Vermont." Charlie had several other titles he used over the years, most of which emphasized the instrument he was best known for playing: the fiddle. "Fiddling Filosofer" and "Violin Wizard" were two common titles he often used. He did a number of pieces he called "violin mimicry," in which he made all manner of sounds emanate from his fiddle—from the sound of a mockingbird to the voice of a small girl reciting "Mary Had a Little Lamb." Taggart would take his fiddle bow apart, spreading the horsehair away from the bow, and place the fiddle between the hair and the bow, with the hair going over all four strings at once. In this position, he could make the fiddle sound like a Scottish bagpipe or imitate a church organ by rolling out the chords of the doxology. Charlie did a number of physical "stunts" with the fiddle, playing it in every conceivable position—even holding the bow in his mouth. Charlie's number-one title, which was also his best-known and best-loved character sketch, was "The Old Country Fiddler." It is important to note that Charlie Taggart's brand of humor and entertaining was not vaudeville or "slapstick" comedy, as other similar artists performed—his presentations were considered tasteful for even the most conservative audiences.

Eventually, the Lovett Bureau sold its interest with Charlie Taggart to Alonzo Foster, head of the Star Lyceum Bureau of New York City. Thus began a working relationship that lasted about ten years. The work with the

Charlie Taggart, helping himself with a bicycle, circa 1905. *Courtesy of the Newbury, Vermont Historical Society.*

Star Bureau was in the wintertime—at least three months per year. From an article that appeared in *Lyceum Magazine*, dated May 1912, an unknown writer said of Charlie Taggart, "Foster has sent him to entertain rich and poor. He has sent Taggart and his festive fiddle to lyceum courses, church affairs, parlor doings, slum benefactions and banquets high in the price and low in the neck. Foster uses more and more of his time, which is the loudest testimonial."

During these months of work in New York, Taggart lived in the Brooklyn area. One known address he was staying at during those years was 863 President Street. Charlie mentioned that he took trumpet lessons from Edwin Franko Goldman, a contemporary of John Philip Sousa. In his rejected *Vermont Life* article from the late 1940s, Charlie remembered his time in "the Big Apple":

> [My] *work was mostly in the city and suburbs. This gave me excellent drill in adaptation of my programs to special groups, such as men's clubs, women's clubs, missions, YMCA's, prisons, insane asylums, battleships, reform schools, private parties, churches* [etc.]. *What to do, and how to do it, was a problem in each case…one of the hardest groups to interest was the poor fellows in the Bowery YMCA…finding a warm place to sit, they went to sleep during the program and had to be shaken awake by the attendants…the holiday season was a busy one for entertainers in New York City, so, during my work there, I seldom got home for the Christmas tree festivities.*

It was during this time that Charlie developed his "cold stage program" in order to deal with the inconsistencies of the many different venues where he performed. An article in *Lyceum Magazine* from May 1912, as well as his publicity materials, described his approach:

> *For dimly lighted rooms, I use more music and fewer impersonations. If I have a bad piano, I skip the real music and prolong my list of novelties…so if it is impossible to adjust your conditions to my work, I simply adjust my work to your conditions. However, if the hall is sufficiently warm for the people to be comfortable, and the stage is sufficiently lighted so they can see every changing expression on my beautiful countenance, and if the piano is on the stage and in good tune, and if the front row of children is dispersed thru the audience with their parents, it will be a delight and a joy to me, and your people will get the best possible results.*

Charlie Taggart at the piano in his home, circa 1900. *Courtesy of the Newbury, Vermont Historical Society.*

During the other nine months of the year, Taggart had to find work with other entertainment bureaus or on his own. He worked for a number of different bureaus all across the country, including the Brockway Bureau in Pittsburgh, Pennsylvania, and the New Dixie Bureau in Columbia, Mississippi. In early 1905, Charlie ventured on a Midwestern tour. He wrote the following about this tour to the editor of the *Groton (Vermont) Times*, which later appeared in that same newspaper:

Amery, Wisconsin
February 3, 1905

Dear friend Lord:
Mrs. Taggart sends me The Times every week and I assure you it is a welcome visitor. The items from the neighboring towns seem vastly more interesting while sitting in a hotel office way out here than when at home. My work for the Chicago Bureau has been thus far in Indiana, Michigan and Wisconsin; next week I go to Iowa. It is pretty cold here, 42 degrees below zero at Rib Lake, Wis. yesterday morning. I took a seven mile drive in the night. Had to buy a cap and mittens and borrow a fur coat. The liveryman covered the floor of the sleigh with hot bricks, and we were none too warm. Lots of foreigners all over the state, mostly German, but a good sprinkling of Scandinavians and others. I struck the iron belt in northern Michigan and had a good chance to see the working of the iron mines. The country looks new, uncultivated. Lots of lumber camps, especially in northern Wisconsin. Plenty of deer, small game, wolves and bears. The game laws are not so strict here as in Vermont. Both bucks and deer may be killed and a month is the time outlawed-November, I think. Most of the desirable Government land has been taken up, but a few people are building them[selves] *shacks and holding their claims. I talked with one man from Indiana, who was returning from his claim. He was a typical woodsman, Indian moosehide moccasins, etc. He said he had to tramp twenty miles on snowshoes to his claim. Lots of hunters from*

Charlie Taggart dressed as a Charles Dickens character, circa 1900. *Courtesy of the Newbury, Vermont Historical Society.*

Chicago go to these parts in the hunting season. Special trains are run for their accommodation. Lots of silver in circulation here-too much to suit me; I prefer bills. I expect to be home about the middle of March. I finish with the Mutual Bureau March 11 at Neptune, Ohio.
I wish you success in your work.

Sincerely,
C.R. Taggart

Loneliness, as Charlie discovered, was simply part of the job, along with hard living conditions. He agonized about being gone for so long at a time from his wife and children, as well as his friends and neighbors. In the unpublished *Vermont Life* article in the late 1940s, he wrote about this Midwestern tour of 1905, saying, "I was thrilled when I anticipated my first trip west, and my first date, Rolling Prairie, Ind., sounded far, far away from Vermont. For ten weeks I never saw a soul that I had ever seen before. Lonesome! I resolved over and over again that when this trip was finished, I would go into some business that would keep me at home. I even did some dreaming about a chicken farm."

In spite of the hardships, Charlie Taggart kept entertaining and continued to perfect his craft. By all accounts, his entertaining was becoming profitable and successful enough that he considered relocating to a different community—one that had a railroad station, saving him the long drive by horse from East Topsham.

Around 1907, Taggart moved his family from East Topsham to Newbury, not far from the Connecticut River. He purchased a home north of the center of the village, which he named Elmbank, for all the elm trees on the property. It had the added benefit of being about one hundred feet from the Newbury depot—a very easy commute. His mother, Emily, as well as his mother-in-law, Sarah Little, came to live with Charlie, Edna and their three girls. Charlie wrote about Elmbank in the unpublished *Vermont Life* article:

Elmbank, our name for our Newbury home, overlooked the railroad station…coming home from these long tours was a joy to me…it was good to get back to [Edna] *and* [our] *three children, and take up my home enjoyments—amateur photography, rifle practice, hunting, mountain climbing and doing odd jobs in my shop. For a time, we had a home orchestra: our three girls and Dad—Miriam on the piano, Evelyn, the trumpet, Elisabeth, the violin, and Dad, slide trombone. We were never*

> *sorry that we picked Newbury for a home. We lived there for more than thirty years. We always considered the view from Mt. Pulaski overlooking the village and the Connecticut River* [to be] *the most beautiful in the state. Mount Moosilauke in New Hampshire was in full view from our house, and with a telescope, we could see the guests at the Tip Top House. One of our favorite outings was a climb to the top* [of Moosilauke], *via the Glen Cliff trail.*

Charles Ross Taggart was beginning to hit his stride and was becoming better known. The demand for "The Man from Vermont" was growing. Many more trips, many more engagements and many more interesting people to meet were all in store. As much as he loved the limelight, he always looked forward to coming home. The following undated poem was written by Charlie while heading home on the train, returning from a southern tour, anticipating his arrival at Elmbank:

Up the Old Connecticut

Up the old Connecticut, the placid old Connecticut,
Clear and still its surface lies below the rushing train.
Showing to perfection
All its borders in reflection,
Tranquil and unruffled in its journey to the main.

Up the old Connecticut, the winding old Connecticut,
Now we leave it far away, with meadows in between
Sometimes strongly sweeping,
Sometimes gently creeping,
Broadly curving southward flows this olden, golden stream.

Up the old Connecticut, historic old Connecticut,
On its bank I'm riding in the twilight of the day,
Flying to my homeland,
My dear Green Mountain homeland;
My back is turned to Dixie, and I'm coming home to stay.

Chapter 3

TRAINS AND AUTOMOBILES

"ALL HAS GONE SMOOTHLY SINCE"

February 21st, 1919
Tawas City, Mich.

To The Redpath Lyceum Bureau
Chicago-Evanston, Illinois

The general impression as to Charles Ross Taggart who appeared here last night seems to be that they packed up their troubles in their old kit sack and smiled, smiled miles of smiles. Some have expressed doubts of being able to put on the facial reverential features for next Sunday morning service. The old fiddle talked right out and said things and all agreed it must be a female fiddle to do all the talking and not let her beau say a word. It was so natural. Just perfectly humanlike. Our doctors wanted to hold a post mortem examination of the piano to see where the talking came from. We have some long haired piano players who play with their hair over their ears and [one of them said] *she never could play with the grace divine of Mr. Taggart.*

Signed,
L.H. Emerson,
Sec. & Treas.

In 1909, Charlie Taggart's letterhead showed four bureaus with which he was affiliated: Lovett, in Boston; Star, in New York; Brockway, in Pittsburgh; and

Charlie Taggart in two different character poses, circa 1910. *Courtesy of the Newbury, Vermont Historical Society.*

New Dixie in Columbia, Mississippi, as well as his home address—Newbury, Vermont. Over the course of his career, he was involved with hundreds of lyceum and Chautauqua bureaus all across the United States and parts of Canada. However, Charlie confided in a letter dated January 23, 1910, to Harry Harrison of the Redpath Bureau that he was getting restless at "the kangaroo method" of hopping from bureau to bureau. Like his earlier days in East Topsham, where he was a jack-of-all-trades farmer, teacher and tinkerer who wanted just one job, Charlie wanted steady work with just one bureau: the Redpath Lyceum and Chautauqua Bureau, headquartered in Chicago, Illinois. The Redpath was considered the best of the best—the best presenters and the best audiences. Charlie had filled some time for Redpath in the past but wanted it to be his one and only bureau. In this same 1910 letter, Charlie implored Harrison: "I feel sure that I can make my work better and better from year to year, and hold my friends among committees and managers and audiences, when we ever get started."

The letter goes on:

> *I do long for the class of people to entertain that you furnish—the representative people of the towns and cities where your men go. A large*

part of this local city work [in New York] *is unsatisfactory, for does it sound like boasting to say that most of the Yankee humor that I put forth does require a little previous knowledge on* [the] *part of the listeners? I never get the guffaw of the ignorant. For an uncultured, illiterate crowd, I make the most of my spectacular work: my tricks and ventriloquism—these go everywhere, so I never fall flat. But before an audience of bright, keen, intelligent people that respect something good—that is when I can get inspiration—new ideas. They bring out the best in me, and honest "hope to die," I never* [fail] *to give satisfaction before such people.*

I ought not to take so much of your time with such an effusion as this, and it really is distasteful to talk so much about myself, but this "Man from Vermont" must be boosted, and I'm his manager, and the dear little Kiddies up in the Green Mountains must have shoes.

Cordially,
C.R. Taggart

Charlie would, indeed, get much work through the Redpath over the next twenty years, and while he still had to "kangaroo" from time to time, he got most of his bookings through it. A contract for the 1913 Chautauqua season shows that Charlie received $115 a week for six performances per week over a two-month period. At the height of his career in the mid-1920s, he was getting $25 a performance, with a minimum of four performances a week, for a twenty-five-week contract per year. Of those twenty-five weeks, generally ten weeks were lyceum work and the remainder Chautauquas. The work was usually broken up into two halves, so it didn't mean twenty-five consecutive weeks on the road. Chautauqua tours were in the summer, where lyceums were generally in the winter or fall. Charlie also had the option of booking dates independently in the New England states, provided that they didn't conflict with his Redpath itinerary.

The chief difference between a lyceum and a Chautauqua—numbers. In the lyceum tours, Charlie was by himself, traveling from one place to another, giving a presentation and then hurrying on to his next destination. Early Chautauquas were similar to lyceums but eventually became a solid circuit in a set number of communities for a set number of weeks, with no free time in between. With the Chautauqua, Taggart was part of a whole company of presenters that toured together for the duration of the circuit, presenting in a particular community for three to five days. Known as "Circuit Chautauqua" or "Tent Chautauqua," these were caravans of political speakers, Prohibition advocates, ministers and

"And still the wonder grew
That one small head could carry all he knew."

As an entertainer, Charles R. Taggart supplies a long-felt want, combining, as he does in himself, the talents of a whole company. His versatility is his strong point. At the same time, every feature of his program shows the effect of study, training and years of experience.

Music. Mr. Taggart is a thorough musician. He has made a specialty of the voice and piano, having studied with the best instructors in the country, including courses at the New England Conservatory of Music, Boston. He has a rich baritone voice; possesses a knack with the banjo; and can transform his violin into anything from a bird song to the human voice. His songs with violin accompaniment are peculiarly pleasing.

Readings. His readings and impersonations are unexcelled. Humor and pathos, the tragic and sublime, all appear in his program. He appreciates a good story himself and can tell one so that others will appreciate it. He has studied at the Emerson College of Oratory.

Ventriloquism. He is an expert ventriloquist, and never fails to awaken wonder and mirth by his mysterious art.

Mr. Taggart is a man of fastidious tastes and high aims, and his entertainments bear the stamp of his own personality. He is highly endorsed by the Y. M. C. A., C. E. Societies, and kindred organizations. He has been five years before the public, and has met everywhere with unqualified success.

occasionally singers and other entertainers. However, entertainers were not always eagerly sought by local Chautauqua sponsors, as the main thrust was education and enlightenment, not necessarily entertainment—unless they came at a low enough price. Chautauqua audiences primarily came for the speakers. Nonetheless, Charlie did get work on several Chautauqua tours, rubbing elbows with the likes of William Jennings Bryan, the orator and statesman, who was one of the most requested and sought-after speakers on the Circuit Chautauqua.

The one additional benefit of the Chautauquas to Charlie was the interaction with fellow presenters, which eased his loneliness. He made many friends on the Circuit Chautauqua over the years. Besides Bryan, he noted a number of then famous speakers and performers of the day, including singers Frederick Wheeler and Elsie Baker,

This page and opposite: Front cover, inside and back of an early Charles Ross Taggart program, circa 1898. *Courtesy of the Newbury, Vermont Historical Society.*

The entertainment given by Charles R. Taggart was in every way satisfactory to those who attended. The house was well-filled by an appreciative audience, and wishes are expressed that Mr. Taggart will come again.—*United Opinion.*

Charles R. Taggart gave a most unique and pleasing entertainment at the Passumpsic Baptist Church last evening. For one man to give an entertainment of an hour and a half as vocalist, musician, reader and impersonator, and hold his audience breathless with admiration is a wonderful thing. His rendering of Poe's "Raven" exceeded in expression and pathos anything I had ever heard.

MRS. S. LOUISE BARTON,
Evangelist and Lecturer, Boston, Mass.

Johnson, Vt., Nov. 7, 1899.
Mr. Charles R. Taggart successfully entertained an audience in Normal School Hall Monday evening.

Mr. Taggart is versatile and whether in dramatic recital, impersonation, ventriloquism, or in songs, he won merited applause.

He is a man of refinement and has much capacity to please a popular audience.

W. E. RANGER,
Principal State Normal School.

Mr. Charles R. Taggart gave a very interesting entertainment in our Chapel last evening. His program was varied and very entertaining, holding the attention of the audience from beginning to end. His rendering of the Scotch dialect was particularly good.

MYRTA E. KNIGHT,
Pres. Montrose Chapel Society.
Wakefield, Mass., Nov. 22, 1900.

Last evening, in the M. E. Church, Charles R. Taggart gave a very acceptable entertainment consisting of readings, impersonations and vocal and instrumental music. The interest of the audience was not allowed to flag for even a moment. The people will eagerly look forward to the next annual visit of Mr. Taggart.

IRVING C. BROWN,
Pastor M. E. Church.
Monroe, N. H., Aug. 27, 1897.

Mr. Taggart has several times entertained Ryegate audiences—his latest appearance here being the present season, when before the Christian Endeavor Society and their friends he rendered a very acceptable program. As he alone can easily fill out an evening with a varied and interesting program we would most heartily recommend Mr. Taggart to all C. E. Societies wishing to give an enjoyable high-grade entertainment.

EDITH B. GIBSON,
Pres. Y. P. S. C. E.
Ryegate, Vt., Dec. 6, 1898.

E. Montpelier, Vt.
Chas. R. Taggart has been with us two evenings and given splendid entertainments to enthusiastic audiences. He is certainly a man of great talent and ability, and all who hear him once will want to hear him again.

[REV.] A. B. ALDRIDGE.

The concert and entertainment given in the vestry of the Presbyterian Church last week Thursday evening by Charles R. Taggart was a fine thing and heartily enjoyed by the small audience present. Arrangements have been made to have Mr. Taggart come again when it is hoped more people will come out to hear him.—*St. Johnsbury Republican.*

Mr. Charles R. Taggart's entertainments are of superior merit. His selections, both musical and literary, display excellent taste and good judgment. Either as vocalist, instrumentalist, or dramatic reader, he never fails to capture his audience. His impersonations are masterpieces and well deserve the hearty applause which they receive.

SAM'L A. JACKSON,
Pastor, Reformed Presbyterian Church.
So. Ryegate, Vt., Feb. 2, 1899.

Thetford, Vt., June 20, 1899.
Mr. Charles R. Taggart recently gave in this place a very pleasing entertainment consisting of readings, impersonations, vocal selections, etc. He easily captivated his audience, and held the closest attention during the evening.

H. N. DUNHAM, Prin. Thetford Academy.

Mr. Chas. R. Taggart gave a most pleasing entertainment before our Y. P. S. C. E. last evening. His rendering of Poe's "Raven," his dialect readings and impersonations were especially good, but all parts of the programme were so good that it was a difficult task to say which was the best. We hope to have Mr. Taggart with us again at a future date.

JOHN RUSSELL HENDERSON,
Pastor Congregational Church.
Roxbury, Vt., Oct. 14, 1899.

Groton, Vermont, June 25, 1900.
Mr. Charles R. Taggart gave his "Ideal Entertainment" in K. of P. hall last Friday evening, June 22, to a large audience. Mr. Taggart has the happy combination of entertaining and instructing, and whose programme is of high order and free from all objectionable features. I cheerfully commend him to all societies who desire a first-class entertainment.

Very truly yours,
C. C. LORD, Editor Groton Times.

To the general public: I can testify to the excellence of Charles R. Taggart's entertainments, both musical and literary. His performances show the character of the man, and while they please the taste, they can but elevate the tone of his audiences and make them better for life and its wonderful uses.

E. W. HATCH, Pastor Cong'l Church.
East Corinth, Vt., Sept. 4, 1897.

One of the best entertainments given in Hyde Park for many a day was that given at the Town Hall last Saturday evening by Mr. Taggart. The entertainment consisted of vocal and instrumental music, readings and ventriloquism, all of the parts being taken by Mr. Taggart and all being well rendered. Mr. Taggart is an artist and gives an entertainment that cannot fail to please. Should he come here again, a full house will be his.—*Morrisville News & Citizen.*

Photographs by Corliss, Newbury, Vt.

...peared in various roles and delightfully entertained the audience with ...gs, readings, piano selections, dialect readings, impersonations, etc.—*Wakefield (Mass.) Daily Item.*

Spanish American War hero Richmond Pearson Hobson, labor leader John Mitchell, arctic explorer Dr. Frederick Cook, minister and orator Dewitt Miller and Shakespearean actor and director Ben Greet, among others. Charlie wrote the following letter while riding on a train in Illinois on February 23, 1921, recounting how several years earlier, at a Chautauqua, he had made the acquaintance of a local newspaper editor who would become a U.S. president:

As I was acquainted with the platform manager, he introduced me to some of the notable people of the town, and it chanced that one evening the platform

> *manager…and I were invited to the home of one of the* [physicians] *of the town to take supper and to meet a few of the town's people. We had a very pleasant time…*[The local editor] *was a good conversationalist, and, in fact, did his full share of the talking at the table…After supper, we… went to the auditorium in the editor's big car. He was a good Chautauqua booster, and introduced the talent from the platform…I recall the event with special interest…the genial editor was Mr. Warren G. Harding, and the town was Marion, Ohio.*

Despite the camaraderie of fellow platformists on the circuit, Charlie still longed to be with home and family, as he writes in an undated letter, circa 1909, which appeared in the *United Opinion*: "This is pleasant, but at times, I envy people who can stay in one place the year round; sleep in one bed; eat regular meals; and be at home all the time. But I reckon we'll all have to stay where Providence places us, 'you in your little corner and I in mine.'"

Taggart had to find contentment and unexpected bonuses in things that he found along the way, as he wrote in the following undated article that appeared in *Lyceum Magazine*:

> *The events of the earlier morning had been very disagreeable, including, as they did, a cold wash in a cold room at 5 a.m.; a vain hunt for a towel; a pilgrimage to the stairway—at a terrible risk of discovery—to call the porter; a greasy breakfast, with overcoat on, eaten in a cold, dimly-lighted room; a jolty, bumpy ride beside a three-hundred-pound drummer, who occupied all his share of the seat, as well as most of mine; and an uncomfortably long wait in a cold room at the* [railroad] *station. But it was all over at last, and I beheld with pleasure the picture which utterly obliterated all the effects of the uncomfortable happenings.*
>
> *Time, six a.m., January 6th. Place, C&O Railroad train going west, on the Kentucky side of the Ohio River, near Cincinnati.*
>
> *A ruddy morning glow in a perfectly clear sky, slowly broadening and lightening behind the black line of rolling hills on the Ohio side of the river. The stream is a beautiful blue, and the reflection of the ruddy sky upon it gives it a golden tinge in places. It is still dark and mysterious in the north and west, but light and wonderful by contrast in the south and east. A few stray sparks from the engine flit past like fireflies through the white smoke, which now and then shuts out the view entirely. The glory of the sky*

CHARLES ROSS TAGGART

He is a Musician, a former student in the New England Conservatory of Music, Boston.

He is a Humorist, a present student in the school of life.

He puts fun into his music, and music into his fun.

He presents humor in musical form.

He fiddles and talks and laughs and sings himself into your life and makes you better.

He absorbs the spirit of real humor from everything and gives it out in bright and new forms.

His rythmic pantomimic sketches using the piano and the violin are good for sore eyes and ears.

All that he does points upwards, leaves a good taste in the mouth and cheers the heart for the sober realities of life.

From a Charles Ross Taggart publicity sheet, circa 1920. *Courtesy of the Newbury, Vermont Historical Society.*

THE MAN FROM VERMONT

Scotch Literature and Music

In his monolog sketch, "Uncle Sandy and the Book Agent," he sings and fiddles a number of characteristic Scotch tunes, and gives a few choice bits from his favorite, Burns.

Ventriloquism

He mystifies and delights his audiences by practicing this deceptive art with the aid of his invisible assistant.

Violin

His mimicry and imitations show what wonderful effects may be produced with this instrument, and the skillful and unique way in which he manipulates the violin always gets the crowd.

Piano

Mr. Taggart studied the piano at the *New England Conservatory of Music* in Boston, and his piano work is always pleasing to music lovers.

Pianologues

Among his clever *original* pianologues are "The Story of a County Fair," which is a rural comedy.

The "Old Soldier's Vision" (patriotic).

"A Burlesque of Poe's Raven," which is a favorite with literary people, and has been appreciated at such gatherings as an alumni meeting of the Emerson College of Oratory, and the International Lyceum Association.

A "Lecture on Classical Music," in which a romantic story with a musical theme is explained and illustrated in a most surprising and side-splitting manner.

He is constantly creating and compiling *New Material,* so his programs are always fresh.

brightens, and now a light orange and yellow is taking the place of the red. The black horizon is fringed with trees, and an occasional tiny square speck of a building, or a sharp-pointed church spire glides out into view. Now the track swings away from the river for a little, and we rush past a cornfield with the stocks of corn crouching in the dusk like motionless sentinels on duty, while in the distance the river looks like a long glittering snake.

Now we are back on its bank again. A river steamer, with its great splashing stern propeller, is making its way slowly up stream, past a long string of coal barges, floating quietly as if anchored in mid-stream. The sky is all aglow now, and the sun almost over the hills. Here he comes; also my station, Cincinnati.

Charlie wrote many letters about his travels to the editors of local papers, becoming a freelance travel correspondent. His letters were published by the hometown papers and eagerly read by many people back in his local vicinity, hoping to catch a verbal glimpse of the world outside of Newbury and perhaps envying the long excursions of "The Man from Vermont."

While on a southern train, en route from Knoxville to Nashville, Tennessee, Charlie shared the following with the readers of the *United Opinion* of Bradford, dated January 16, 1907:

Editor, United Opinion,

As so many requests were given me to send letters through your paper, while I was home recently, I will while away a few moments just now by sharing some of the [impressions] *I have been getting on this ride.*

It looked cloudy this morning when the train left Knoxville (at 9:30), and I expected a rainy day and I didn't much care, as I thought the trip would be monotonous at best, and it is just as enjoyable riding through an uninteresting, dismal country in the rain as in the sunshine. There is a certain coziness about a comfortable railroad car with pleasant passengers [inside] *and rain outside. A good place to read and doze and sleep and wake and stretch and watch the drops run down the window pane and think how much nicer it is to be inside than to be outside, but I have been disappointed. In the first place, it stopped raining soon after we started, and the sun came out. In the second place, the ride has not been monotonous. I hadn't looked over my map sufficiently to notice that the route led directly over and through the Cumberland mountains, and the scenery is almost, if not quite equal to that through the Blue Ridge from Salisbury to Knoxville.*

Wonderful! In certain places, the railroad follows the principle I used to use with my grandfather's old mare: get up a good galloping speed down one hill so to carry us up the next.

The mountains are covered with forests of oak with scattered trees of pine, white birch and holly. The bunches in the tops of the trees, which I mistook at first for crows' nests, I found to be mistletoe. Plenty of it here. But my! You ought to see the little towns (?) the train stops at. Cassville is nowhere. And the people!—"Mountain whites," you have read about them. Men [in] *slouch hats and leggings for horse-back riding in clothes "pre-Adamite in cut," some with rifles for hunting (I'm not quite far enough west for the cartridge belt and six-shooters).*

But most of the men and boys seem to be on a strike: hands in their pockets or whittling sticks. Most of the women seem to be sitting or standing in the doors of the log cabins, and most of the children wave and shout to the train. But the scenery is grand, beyond description, so I won't attempt it, but I frequently forget what I was going to say for gazing so long from the window.

At dinner time, the train stopped in the woods, where all I could see was the station and one house, which must have been a hotel, for the conductor shouted, "Twenty minutes for dinner." By the way, about an hour back, the brakeman took the number of those who wanted dinner, so the whole train load—conductor, brakeman, engineer and all—went over to the hotel for dinner. The engineer sat at my elbow, so I ate in peace, knowing the train would stay as long as he did.

The conductor seemed a little anxious, I thought, lest somebody would run off with the train, and finished quickly and went to watch it. It was a fine dinner: potatoes, both kinds; chicken; lima beans; cabbages, etc.; all passed from one to another around the table, like "pass the key."

Well, this seems to be about all of interest that I can think of just now, unless it be the pigs, but you have all seen pigs, so I don't need to mention them, but it isn't considered proper in Vermont for an old mother pig and her devoted brood to go about unprotected all over the country, which seems to be so common an occurrence here as to be unnoticed… While walking the street in Knoxville the other evening, the strains of "Everybody Works but Father" floated out of a shooting gallery, so I stepped inside and drank it in. It sounded so natural, but I might mention one thing which is a great relief: I haven't seen a "Cremo Cigar" sign for three whole days.

Very truly,
C.R. Taggart

Traveling by car was sometimes a necessity, as passenger trains didn't operate on Sundays, were often delayed and didn't go everywhere one needed to go. Charlie had several experiences riding in early automobiles, including the following account of how he got from Farrington to Fort Madison, Iowa, dated August 8, 1910, which must have surely amused readers of the *United Opinion*:

> *As my Farrington engagement was on a Saturday night, and as Sunday trains were scarce, it was necessary to make the trip of 30 miles by auto.*
>
> *We started at 9:30 p.m., as soon as I had finished my work, in a monster Thomas touring car. Three gentlemen and one lady (the driver's wife) went just for the ride, besides the driver. (I can't recall the spelling of the other word, so we will say "driver").*
>
> *We started off admirably with a "Heigh ho! Let 'er go!" creeping, bumping, bounding, swiftly, recklessly in and out among the carriages and foot men who were leaving the grounds. It took many a toot from our big, round eyed monster to clear the way, but at length we shot out with a rush into the road, and away we went, faster and faster, till the telephone poles shot past us like they do when seen from a* [train] *car window. Passing teams* [caused] *heart-gripping moments. One hardly breathes until we pass. But the teams were soon left behind, and we had the road to ourselves. How we strained our eyes to see as far as the long stream of light would reach!*
>
> *We learned, after several water bars, bridges, trolley and railroad tracks were crossed, to make preparations for the jumps. The first one or two of these were very surprising. I soared into the air like a bird, and lit all over my violin case, suitcase, and the man beside me; nearly lost my hat and grazed my shins. I asked one of the men if he had any idea how fast we were going. He glanced at the speedometer and said, "40 miles an hour." I believed him. But this did not last always. Oh no! Things began to happen.*
>
> *First, the lights went out and we came to a dead stop, and 15 minutes were spent before we could start. Then, after a few more miles, a great smoking was seen in front, and it was discovered that water was needed to cool the engine (I believe that was the matter).*
>
> *"Here, Joe, we passed a farmhouse a bit back. Turn back and borrow a bucket and get some water."*

Opposite: From the inside of a Charles Ross Taggart publicity sheet, circa 1925. *Courtesy of the Newbury, Vermont Historical Society.*

FIDDLING!

"Mr. Taggart opened his program with what he called his 'Acrobatic Fiddle,' playing it in every conceivable position, even holding the bow in his mouth, and the 'Old Country Fiddler' sketch kept the audience in fits of laughter from start to finish."—**Towanda, Pa.**

"He has his fiddle tamed If he wants it to do something it was never created to do, it does it.

"Under his manipulation the Fiddle talks. It sings the songs of birds."—**Daily Banner, Greencastle, Ind.**

"His Fiddle imitations are wonderful. We liked best his 'Church Organ,' when he played on all four strings at once, rolling out the grand chords of the Doxology."

—**Paducah, Ky., Evening Sun.**

VICTOR, COLUMBIA AND EDISON RECORDS

From Ross Taggart's records he draws much pleasing platform material.

"The Country Fiddler" records include, besides the fiddle tunes, rollicking stories, including discussions by the Old Fiddler of Modern School Methods, Book Agents, Crime Treatment, Woman's Suffrage, The County Fair, The Pineville Wedding, The Pineville Band, and The Pineville School Board.

* * * * *

COMMENT

"Mr. Edison thinks your work is excellent."—W. H. Miller, Recording Laboratories, New York City.

Ross Taggart's early activities included several terms as a country school teacher in the little red school houses ot Vermont—farming—clerking in a country grocery store—teaching singing schools—giving lessons in violin and piano. He has been a student in the New England Conservatory of Music, and the Emerson College of Oratory, Boston. He is best known by his distinguished platform work in America. He has been with the Redpath Lyceum and Chautauqua Bureau for more than twenty years, and has given more than four thousand programs in nearly every State in the Union.

Joe and one of the passengers trotted off. Soon, we heard a pump handle working vigorously, while a dog barked furiously, and soon the water was brought and poured into the proper place. Three bucketfuls were necessary, then we started again. The cranking occupied about five or ten minutes each time we stopped. Joe always worked at it till he gave out, then the driver jumped out and set it buzzing with one or two turns.

The driver spent most of his time telling how quick we would have been there if he had only taken the "Buick" instead of this old rattletrap.

Something seemed to be the matter with the clutching apparatus, for every time the gear was changed, such a tremendous rattling set up that it seemed that something must bust presently. Well, the most serious incident was when we ran out of gasoline or rather, when the machine did, three miles before we reached Fort Madison. We were right in the woods and there we "sot and sot" for four hours, and it began to rain. Heigh ho, people! Didn't we have a time of it?

"Joe, how much gasoline was there in the tank when we started?"

Joe: "Five gallons."

"Sure?"

"Sure."

"You filled it?"

"I saw it put in."

"Well boys, here we are."

"If I ever take this machine out again!"

"Three cheers for the Thomas Flier!"

"Joe, you'll have to go find some kerosene. I guess we can go in on that. Must be a farm house somewhere near here."

So Joe and one of the men take off one of the lamps for a light and start off into the woods—we wait ten, fifteen minutes, half an hour, telling jokes, singing snatches of songs, laughing at the novelty of the adventure.

"What time does your train go?" asks the driver.

"Seven, fifty-seven a.m."

"Oh well, we'll make it. Ha! ha! ha!"

A light appears coming slowly. Then subdued voices, then the glimmer of a can carried between two people.

"Gasoline or coal oil?"

"Coal oil."

"Well, we'll try it." They did.

"Crank 'er up, Joe."

After Joe gives it up, puffing and blowing, the driver gets out and sends it buzzing, but it buzzes slower and slower and stops.

He does it again, and again, same result.

"Guess the engine got too cold on us."

Long breaths. Rain still pattering on the roof. Muddy feet, wet people climb in to rest and think it over.

"Well, Joe, better go up to the farm-house and 'phone the livery at Ft. Madison to send us some gasoline."

The wet man volunteers to go back. Joe stays and works, trying to get the kerosene out of the tank. Driver says, "the gasoline and kerosene won't work together. Gasoline mighty exclusive...wants no company. Will work alone or not at all."

Wet man comes back bye and bye.

"Did you get 'em?"

"Yes. They will start just as soon as they can hitch up and draw the gasoline. Farmer up to the house says he's going to bed now." All laugh.

Nothing to do but wait and listen to Joe under the machine rattling away.

Joe: "I can't get this blamed valve open!"

Driver gets down and helps him and finally the tank is freed from the kerosene that wouldn't work.

We wait. Rain still drips. Silence.

I sleep a little.

A twist as somebody changes position.

One hour passes—no livery team.

Somebody says, "Guess that man must have got the wrong road."

"Did you tell him where we were?"

"Yes, oh yes, I told him all right."

Another hour.

At last, wheels!—the team.

"Hello! Where have you been all this time?"

"I got to sleep and let the kid drive and he got off the road two or three miles."

"Oh."

Well, the livery man is paid and the tank filled, the machine cranked, and with tremendous burr, we are off, arriving at Fort Madison at 4 a.m.

All has gone smoothly since.

Chapter 4

GOING SOME

"THEY SEEMED TO APPRECIATE MY BRAND OF HUMOR"

Charles R. Taggart
Activities When Not Lecturing—is Proud of His Garden—Photography His Hobby
*(*Lyceum Magazine, *October 1913)*

Newbury, Vermont, Charles R. Taggart's home, is a small but picturesque and historic village on the B.&M. R.R. between Boston and Montreal. It overlooks the fair and fertile meadows of the Coos country, and nestles under the shadow of Mt. Pulaski, from whose summit one commands a view of the Connecticut Valley for miles. There are no manufacturing interests in Newbury, and the people are mostly descendants of the old Puritan stock of New England.

Mr. Taggart's home, "Elmbank," is on a bluff overlooking the railroad track and Mt. Pulaski on the west, and the Connecticut River on the east. The grounds cover about an acre in which grow twenty-five elm trees. The house is over a hundred years old, but is not conspicuous on this account, as there are many houses in this beautiful old village which date back further than this one. From the lawn, the Connecticut [River] *and the New Hampshire mountains can be seen...the Franconias, the old Mount Moosilauke, 4,800 ft. high...It takes as much hustling in Mr. Taggart's vacation time to make connections between his various duties and pleasures as it does in his Chautauqua season to make railroad connections. He is head gardener on the estate and justly proud of his lettuce and radishes, corn and beans, peas, potatoes, cabbages and other good things. Workmen are hard to find and Mr. Taggart has grown used to turning his hand to most anything that is needed about the house—carpentering, painting, papering or cementing. The bank of the hill near his house is thickly wooded and for the last three years, he has spent a good deal of time in transforming it into a park with winding paths and rustic seats.*

Besides Mr. and Mrs. Taggart, the family consists of three daughters: Evelyn, Miriam and Elisabeth, aged sixteen, fourteen, and six; Mr. Taggart's

Charles Ross Taggart, with daughter Elisabeth, on their Elmbank property in Newbury, Vermont, circa 1913. *Courtesy of Adam Boyce.*

mother and Mrs. Taggart's mother. They are all lovers of the mountain top and usually find time to climb Moosilauke at least once a year.

Mr. Taggart's hobby is photography, and when he is not doing anything else, he is always taking pictures. His specialty is landscapes. Fishing has never appealed to him, but he always catches the hunting fever when exposed.

Charlie Taggart's entertaining took him all over the country. He was in Pittsburgh, Pennsylvania, during the great flood of 1907 and paid a half-drunken man a quarter to carry him piggyback to a makeshift boat. In Alabama, Charlie wrote about segregation in the South, remarking that railroad cars marked "colored" and "white" were "rather annoying." In Davidson, Tennessee, he had to travel to his next appointed appearance sitting on the front of a motorized flat-topped rail car that was used by the railroad repair crew—his feet dangling over the front, holding on with his left hand, while his right arm cradled his fiddle case and grip. Charlie wrote of visiting Detroit, Michigan, and marveled at seeing the Ford Motor plant, which he wrote put out one thousand cars in an eight-hour day. He visited Postumville, Battle Creek, where he observed the production of Postum and Grape Nuts. In Cynthiana, Kansas, he learned about the different tobacco types and grades while attending a tobacco auction. Charlie endured an extended visit to Aberdeen, South Dakota, where he was snowbound for several days. He wrote, "One of the most spectacular rides I ever took was from Cedar City, Utah, to St. George, Utah, eighty miles with a Mormon priest," admitting, "The Mormon people didn't laugh much, but seemed a very quiet, respectful audience, some like the [Scandinavian] audiences in Wisconsin and Minnesota." He further added, "I used to pat myself on the back because I got the best reaction from intelligent audiences, college groups, etc. They seemed to appreciate my brand of humor."

Charlie wrote the following while on the train in Michigan on February 26, 1919: "Last night, I slept in Petosky, where I could hear the waves of Lake Michigan splashing the shore, and to-night I will sleep at Alpena, within a stone's throw of Lake Huron."

In 1906, he wrote about being "in Old Kentucky," saying, "Kentucky mud! Well, it's as near like Portland cement, mixed, ready for use, as anything I can imagine. I slip and slide around in it, and nearly lost my balance once in getting [from] the station to the hotel."

Charlie made his "shortest jump between lyceum dates," according to a *Lyceum Magazine* article, circa 1915, that said, "The distance was but two and one-half miles—from Conrad to Beaman, Ia.—which he says he would have walked if he had not been laden down with two heavy grips."

In contrast, on August 21, 1911, for the *United Opinion*, Charlie wrote:

> *Just out of curiosity, I did a little reckoning this forenoon, and discovered that I have averaged over five hundred miles of travel for every date filled which (excuse slang) is "going some."*
>
> *My longest jump between dates was 801 miles—Rockport, Mo., to Greenfield, Ohio—and the shortest, 188 miles—Webster City, Iowa to Malvern, Iowa.*

About Scranton, Pennsylvania, in 1905, he wrote, "Of all the places in the world where I don't want to live, this is the one, the first choice. Hills, to be sure, but of coal dust instead of native soil, and I was told the very ground was liable to cave in any time and swallow up whatever happened to be on it."

Charlie witnessed some rather infamous figures, such as Chester Gillette, the young man accused of murdering girlfriend Grace Brown in the Adirondacks of New York State in 1906. The trial, held in Herkimer, was arguably one of

A publicity brochure of Charles Ross Taggart, circa 1910, showing all the many and varied characters he portrayed. It is believed he took all of these images himself. *Courtesy of the Redpath Chautauqua Bureau collection, University of Iowa Libraries, Iowa City.*

the trials of the century, captivating the public's attention worldwide. Charlie was in Herkimer just after the trial, and observed the following:

Dec. 12, 1906

Editor, United Opinion:

Perhaps your readers would like to follow me through a part of a day which has been rather interesting in a way. I had been quietly writing letters in the R.R. station at Herkimer, N.Y. this morning and had just risen from my seat to mail a letter when quite a number of people, mostly men, entered the waiting room and I became aware that something unusual was happening by the whisperings and pointing of fingers. Then I caught the name "Gillette," then I remembered that he was to be taken from Herkimer to Auburn today to await electrocution during the week of Jan. 28, and here he was within four feet of me.

He was conducted by two sheriffs and followed by a train of reporters. The station began to fill very rapidly and the crowd pressed close around to get a glimpse. The poor fellow looked pale but otherwise quite as any other young fellow might. He was well dressed, had rather uncertain eyes and a very ordinary face, not striking in any particular [way], *and seemed quite at his ease. Somebody offered him a cigar which he smoked, but the crowd pressed so hard I soon drew back.*

The reporters bent their heads to catch every word or syllable that escaped him; their hats almost touched his as they scratched away with pencil and tablet.

Presently a man came in whom I found out was a Methodist minister; the crowd broke to let him up, and the prisoner arose and shook his hand, saying, "Goodbye." People got on seats and tables and leaned on each other's shoulders to get a glimpse of the unfortunate boy's face (he seemed hardly more than a boy)...

News of his presence evidently had gone ahead, for at every station there were crowds hoping to get a glimpse. Some of the funny men tried to deceive the crowd by pointing at each other and saying with their lips, "That's him." At Syracuse, the crowd was dense, and the police had their hands full, but the car was switched on to the Auburn train so the crowd missed seeing him leave the car as they expected he would do.

Our train sped on to Rochester, and Gillette went to Auburn to await death or a new trial.

Emotions of various kinds were called up by the sad scene. One old lady in our car went back to look at him. "Why," she said on her return, "he's only a boy. Too bad."

"Mr. Taggart at work in his Studio" at Elmbank in Newbury, Vermont, circa 1910. *Courtesy of the Newbury, Vermont Historical Society.*

> *It seems right that human sympathy should be expressed for the man or boy as an individual, but if he is guilty of the awful crimes he is accused of, no body of people social, civil, judicial or otherwise should say a word to interfere with the just punishment the crime merits.*
>
> *How curious the public is to see a criminal. I believe most people would go farther to see a very bad man than a very good one. Is it because very good people are more numerous? It would be nice to think so. I can't help following with interest the misfortunes of this young man after having seen him.*

Charlie performed twice at the Matteawon, New York Hospital for the Criminally Insane and both times came face-to-face with another notorious personality, namely Henry K. Thaw, who murdered the famous architect Stanford White in 1906. Taggart noted, in his unpublished *Vermont Life* article from the late 1940s, that Thaw "sat in the front seat among the patients. He looked rather bored."

Charlie's work sometimes involved entertainment in asylums of various types. His audition for the Lovett Entertainment Bureau was at an insane hospital. In Northampton, Massachusetts, Charlie gave sixteen different programs for the Northampton Insane Hospital. The following is Charlie's description of an interesting episode at that institution, circa 1914:

> *The patients are marched in to the tune of a march, played on the pipe organ, men and women on opposite sides of the room, with uniformed attendants, in order.*
>
> *Once, as I was watching them file out after my show was over, a female [patient] started for the stage full tilt, with three or four attendants after her. She shouted, "I know him!" and they caught her just as she reached the steps of the platform.*
>
> *The tension was relieved!*

Years later, in the proposed *Vermont Life* article, Charlie Taggart added, "I asked the doctors the next morning at breakfast what she was after. They said, 'She probably wanted to embrace you.'"

At the asylum in Concord, New Hampshire, after one of Charlie's programs, an elderly female patient walked to the stage and handed him her handkerchief, saying, "It's all I have to give you."

Another event remembered by Charlie in later years occurred in Palmer, Massachusetts, at the Epileptic Hospital: "Dr. Flood...said 'Don't be disturbed if some of the patients have to be taken out during your program.' One man collapsed during my burlesque of [Edgar Allan] Poe's Raven; too much for him, apparently."

Charlie gave a program "in a sort of mission in Chicago" where he said, "There was an unruly set of young hoodlums in the front row, and before the superintendent introduced me, he addressed the kids: 'Now, if you boys don't behave yourselves, Mr. Taggart is going to throw you right through that window.' I had that unfortunate speech to overcome. Usually the introductions were appropriate."

At Bob Jones College in Cleveland, Tennessee, "the whole group of students [was] asked to rise and repeat the 'Apostles' Creed' before I was presented. In that sacred atmosphere, I rather looked for a subdued response to my effort, but what was my surprise when they laughed and applauded with vim and in the right places; you could hear a pin drop, such was the quiet between the outbursts."

Although not generally political, Charlie took the opportunity to state his own preference for president, in a letter to the *United Opinion*, written while in Tama, Iowa, in August 1912:

A publicity photo of Charles Ross Taggart, c. 1910, just after he had become affiliated with the Redpath Lyceum and Chautauqua Bureau of Chicago, Illinois, his primary employer for many years. *Courtesy of the Redpath Chautauqua Bureau collection, University of Iowa Libraries, Iowa City.*

I'm sure you will pardon just a word concerning this political situation, even if I disagree with your editorial attitude. Edward Amherst Ott said in his lecture last week, "I would rather be understood two minutes than to be loved all day." I can imagine Mr. [Theodore] *Roosevelt saying that. Many of my friends who were formerly Roosevelt supporters have turned against him, because they attribute his intense earnestness in this new movement to motives of selfishness, egotism, and personal ambition. I must confess I cannot see how, in the light of all the facts in Mr. Roosevelt's life, as one may know them (if he does not), any person can misjudge him thus.*

I believe him to be a courageous, loyal, patriotic man, abundantly fitted to be the leader of this new movement for righteous government, and I would like to see my native State fall into line with these other great States of the West in the Progressive movement.

There! I've said what has been burning to come out, and I feel better.

Taggart was also a strong advocate for national Prohibition. In 1914, he wrote, "We have a strong foe to fight, friends, in our struggle for Nation-Wide Prohibition," and later, while in Schoolcraft, Michigan in 1915, he added, "I heard a rousing Anti-Saloon speech at the Y.M.C.A. in Grand Rapids last Sunday. Michigan people are not discouraged by the results in Ohio. I hope Vermont will show with a big majority where she stands. Let all Vermonters who hate sin and love righteousness watch the saloon and see which side of the disputed question it supports, and vote on the other side."

During World War I, Charlie Taggart, along with other performers, entertained soldiers on the home front, especially those recuperating in hospitals. The following account, written by Charlie in Biblical style, tells of one such performance at Camp Custer in Michigan:

Chronicles of the Camps
by
Charles Ross Taggart
*(*Lyceum Magazine, *January 9, 1918)*

Now it came to pass in the days of Woodrow the King, that a company of singers and players from the islands of the sea, called Hawaiians, together with a man of great stature from the land of Vermont, who was skilled in the use of stringed instruments, went unto the camp called Custer, which is a Sabbath day's journey from Battle Creek, Michigan, to play and make a loud noise before the mighty men of war who had assembled themselves together at that place to prepare for conflict with the powers of darkness.

Now, after that they had played skillfully before these men, behold, there came unto them a goodly man from the tribe of the Y.M.C.A. who spake unto them, saying, "Will ye not come also unto the needy and afflicted, even unto the Base Hospital and make music and mirth for the sick ones? Peradventure it may do them good, and cause them to overcome for a time the temptation to consider too deeply of their evil condition."

Then all the singers and players, together with the Man from the Hill Country of Vermont, spake unto the messenger, saying, "We will go." So, after they had eaten and drunken, they were ready.

Now, as the distance whither they went was great, they were carried thither by a certain man, who was going that way in a chariot which is called by the Americans an automobile, even a Cadillac; and by means of this assistance, they were soon at their journey's end.

Now it came to pass, that as they alighted from the chariot, the man of God, even the Y.M.C.A. secretary, met them and led them to the wards, even to the men who were sick, and could not so much as arise, and said unto them, "Behold! I have brought unto you certain singers and players, who, out of the goodness of their hearts, have laid aside their own pleasures, and have come to make a loud noise upon their instruments and to make merry before you."

Then were the sick men glad in their hearts, and cried out, saying, "Go to it!" And they did so, going about from ward to ward for the space of two hours or thereabouts. And all the sick men, together with the multitude of righteous and comely women who ministered unto them, rejoiced, and spake, saying, "Ye have dealt with us kindly, in coming unto us."

Then all the singers and players sat down to meet with the captains and centurions and mighty men of valor in that place, and supped bountifully. And after that they had eaten, they were carried away in another chariot, even an ambulance. And they were all happy, and did rejoice together, seeing that they had done this thing.

Chapter 5

PHONOGRAPHS AND PHONOFILMS

"The Man from Vermont"
(author unknown, from Lyceum Magazine, December, 1918*)*

Who is funny? Who is clever?
Who is unique and failing never?
Who could keep you laughing ever?
Who is nothing of a braggart?

Who's original as thunder?
Who steals no one else's plunder?
Who, with mirth bursts bands asunder?
Hist, it rimes!—His name is Taggart!

Charlie Taggart was coming up in the world. Besides being a popular fixture on the Redpath circuits, he began to use the new technology of the early twentieth century to enhance his career, becoming a recording and film star. Upon the suggestion of Frederick Wheeler, a singer with whom Charlie toured in the early 1910s, he decided to record many of his "Old Country Fiddler" and "Pineville Folks" monologues for the enjoyment of the public. Charlie went to the Victor Talking Machine headquarters in Camden, New Jersey, on several occasions, eventually making over forty recordings on their label. He also recorded on the Columbia, Edison and Brunswick labels—a recording career that ran from 1914 through 1927.

A cartoon sketch of Charlie Taggart, circa 1915, by an unknown artist named "Packard," which appeared in *Lyceum Magazine*. *Courtesy of the Newbury, Vermont Historical Society.*

"It was a very satisfactory and profitable venture," wrote Charlie, in the late 1940s. He continues describing his work with Victor in his unpublished *Vermont Life* article:

> *Making records for the Victor Phonograph Co. was a new adventure. Had some very nervous moments in making my first audition. At that time… they were glad of unique material, so I got a contract for a certain number of records per year. That kept me busy thinking up new stories for my "Old Country Fiddler," so I sat many hours in trains with my watch, timing the stories and fiddle tunes—so many minutes for ten inch records, and so many more for twelve inch ones.*

Charlie told more about his recording career in his 1927 interview in the *Vermonter*, saying, "While I was under contract with the Victor people, I could not take on other work, and during this time, I had to turn down several very good offers from other companies. I was fearful, at the time, that I'd never have such munificent offers again, but, for some reason, I did."

The image of the Victor dog, Nipper, listening to "His Master's Voice," became part of Charlie's letterhead, and he also listed all twelve Redpath Bureau offices across the United States with which he was affiliated. He sent the following circular to local committees, hoping to boost record sales where he was about to appear, circa 1918:

> *Lyceum or Chautauqua Committee*
> *Gentlemen:-*
>
> *I am to entertain in your city soon. Now would it not be a good plan for you to see the dealers that handle the "Victor Talking Machine" goods and see if they will get out a special ad for my records?*
>
> *It seems to me that it will boost the entertainment as well as the sale of records.*
>
> *I just offer this as a suggestion.*
>
> *Cordially yours,*
> *C.R. Taggart*

Charlie's success with his recordings prompted him to ask for an increase in his Redpath pay, as the following communication from the Redpath office to local managers indicates:

Charles Ross Taggart as "The Old Country Fiddler," circa 1920, in a publicity shot that was featured on the front cover of the *Vermonter* magazine in November 1927.

Bulletin to all the Managers.
Evanston, Nov. 28th, 1916

Dear Fellows:
Taggart: He wants us to keep him on the list and book him without guarantee at $25.00 per date. Will you kindly let me know how many of the fellows will keep him on the list. He certainly made mighty big this year and his reputation is increasing right along through his Victor records. They are constantly increasing his price per record, and now they are paying him a bonus to make records exclusively for them, as the Columbia people are anxious to make records of this kind of entertainment.

Sincerely yours,
H.P. Harrison

Charlie would also make his mark in the talking movie realm, several years before Al Jolson appeared in *The Jazz Singer*. Dr. Lee DeForest, dubbed "The Father of American Radio" due to his invention of the Audion tube, was Charlie's old classmate from Mount Hermon. DeForest, who had many scientific achievements, had also been working on putting sound with moving pictures. In his 1927 *Vermonter* interview, Charlie remembered his short "talkie" career with DeForest:

> *I wrote to Lee DeForest...to congratulate him upon his success in the scientific world. Incidentally, I told him what I had been doing since we were in the same classroom in Old Recitation Hall. DeForest asked me, in reply to my letter, to visit his laboratory and make some tests for his new Phonofilm invention, upon which he was working. The first picture was "The Old Country Fiddler at* [the] *Singing School," and was shown for the first time for a week in the Rialto Theatre in New York City. I was "crazy" to see it, so I stayed over until it was produced, and slipped in five or six times to watch myself. I got more nervous before the picture came on to the screen than I do when I go on the platform in person. It gave me a brand new thrill, and I value new thrills today. Since then I have done other things for Mr. DeForest along this line of work, and these* [Phonofilms], *where the acting is accompanied by the voice, have been shown all over America.*

There seems to be some difference of opinion as to exactly when Charlie's film premiered. The Wikipedia and Silent Era websites cite that it appeared, along with eighteen other Phonofilms, on April 12, 1923. However, the following letter from Lee DeForest to Charlie Taggart, found in the Redpath Collection of the University of Iowa at Iowa City, indicates it was 1924:

> *De Forest Phonofilms, Inc.*
> *220 West 42nd St.*
> *New York*
> *Lee De Forest, President*
> *April 24, 1924*
>
> *Mr. C.R. Taggart*
> *Newbury*
> *Vermont*

Dear Mr. Taggart,
It gives me great pleasure to inform you that your Phonofilm production of "The Old Country Fiddler" was an unqualified success. It never failed to receive enthusiastic response from each audience at the Rialto Theatre, where your quaint and wholesome human was keenly appreciated.

We hope to have an opportunity of making productions of some of your other material at an early date.

Respectfully yours,
Lee De Forest

[P.S.] *Here is the list of cities they gave me at the Phonofilm office, where* [the] *picture had been shown:*
New York, Providence RI, Milwaukee, Passuic NJ, Newark NJ, Duluth, St. Louis, Kansas City, Minneapolis, St. Paul, Pittsburg, Detroit, Boston.

Charles Ross Taggart, in his regular clothes, from the front of a Redpath circular, circa 1920. *Courtesy of the Redpath Chautauqua Bureau collection, University of Iowa Libraries, Iowa City.*

Charlie Taggart also made a few appearances on radio, according to his unpublished *Vermont Life* article, in which he stated, "Radio, as a means of disseminating my material, came in very pat when regular tours became fewer. I worked on several stations, both NBC and Columbia in New York, and also in Davenport, Iowa; Lansing, Mich.; Shenandoah, Iowa and Asheville, N.C."

It seemed as if Charlie was getting better known and might have even taken a different career path, according to the following letters between him and the Redpath bureau :

May 29th, 1919

Dear Mr. Crotty:
I have just had a communication from Mr. Harry Ross Minor, asking for prices, etc. for a trip on the Pacific coast. I had an idea that he was the Redpath man there, but Redpath is not on his stationary. Will this conflict with my work for Redpath? Of course I would like to keep with you even on the Pacific coast, and still I would like the trip. Please let me hear from you concerning the matter.

Cordially,
C.R. Taggart

His proposition is for 1920 & 1921.

Crotty's response:

June 11th, 1919

Mr. C.R. Taggart
c/o LaSalle Hotel
Chicago, Illinois

Dear Friend Taggart:
...I have already written you in regard to the Minor business, and I hope you will not do anything with him. If you do, it will necessitate [our] *not booking you in this or any other Redpath territory.*

Best wishes,
L.B. Crotty

Because of Charlie's loyalty to the Redpath, he didn't pursue the venture further, but it does pose the question: if he *had*, would it have changed his future? Might he have gone on to Hollywood? Well, according to at least one letter to the Redpath, titled "En Route to San Francisco," dated November 1, 1921, Charlie apparently did make it to California, noting, "We ran into a [herd] of cows [with the train] and killed 7, so we are held up a while for repairs."

In the same letter, he wrote, "My mother is so poorly I do not care for a long season next winter and would like plenty of time for my work in the east."

Charlie's mother, Emily (Divoll) Taggart, arguably his biggest fan, and the one who recognized and nurtured his vast talents through the years, died December 29, 1922, and was laid to rest in the Oxbow Cemetery in Newbury, Vermont.

Take A Walk
by Charles R. Taggart
*(*Lyceum Magazine, *1917)*

If you're feelin' kind o' blue,
Take a walk.
If your conscience troubles you,
Take a walk.
It will free you from distraction
When you get your legs in action—
Take a walk.

When you strike a town that's wet,
Take a walk.
As far away as you can get,
Take a walk.
Get up on an elevation,
Pray for all the population;
Take a walk.

If you strike a bum hotel,
Take a walk.
If your room contains a smell,
Take a walk.
Drop your grips and exit quick,

A five-mile hike will do the trick;
Take a walk.

If your wifey failed to write,
Take a walk.
There's another mail to-night,
Take a walk.
Read the one she wrote you last,
Ponder over pleasures past;
Take a walk.

It will do you lots o' good to
Take a walk.
It will help digest your food to
Take a walk.
Honest doctors all advise it,
Every man of wisdom tries it—
Take a walk!

Chapter 6

"UP THE STUMP," BUT NEVER TOO OLD TO LEARN

Elmira, N.Y., May 1, 1914
A Tribute to Mark Twain
(by C.R. Taggart)

Dear Opinion Readers,
On a hill east of Elmira, and overlooking the city, is a little round house, twelve or fifteen feet in diameter, with a chimney and fireplace on one side.

This little retreat was built to stand the weather, and altho' it was built in 1874, is yet in excellent condition. Large plate glass windows all 'round, a flight of steps leading up to the door. The roof is [conical] *and crowned by an appropriate ornament. Inside this cozy little house are two comfortable chairs, a couch, and a round table.*

A flight of rustic steps leads up through a tangle of bushes to the little house, and a little graveled path completely encircles it.

From the west windows, nearly the whole city of Elmira can be seen, and the hill beyond. A most charming outlook! Absolute quiet prevails at the little house, except for the bird songs and occasional lowing of cattle and bleating of sheep from neighboring farms.

The interest which I am sure you all will have in this little round house is all reflected from the personality of its former occupant.

This little house on the hill top was Mark Twain's summer study for a number of years. Here he wrote those delightful stories of his own boyish homes in Hannibal, [Missouri], *"Tom Sawyer" and "Huckleberry*

Finn"; also "The Prince and [the] *Pauper," "The Tramp Abroad," "Life on the Mississippi," "A* [Connecticut] *Yankee at King Arthur's Court," and a part of "Roughing It," besides a number of the short stories.*

As I had time between trains, I walked up there from Elmira this morning (about a mile and a half), and had a most delightful visit with Mrs. Susan Crane, a sister-in-law of Mark Twain. She is a beautiful old lady, hair snowy white, and her home, the old Langdon homestead, and the home of Olivia Langdon, Mark Twain's wife, is there near the little round house. She was pleased to show me many interesting things concerning her distinguished brother-in-law.

She loved to talk of the serious side of him; and I learned that altho' not holding any definite religious belief during most of his life, at the close, he gave a great deal of thought to the reality of religion.

He was entirely devoted to his family, and in the church yard, he has placed this touching sentiment in German to his wife on her tombstone: "Gott sei dir gnädig, O meine Wonne!" [translation: "God be merciful to you, O my joy!"]

In Woodland Cemetery, here in Elmira, in the Langdon lot, stand four plain stones all alike, for Samuel Langhorne Clemens, his wife, Olivia, and his two daughters, Olivia and Jean. He has one daughter still living.

Mark Twain has been called the most truly American writer of them all. He was absolutely sincere; hated hypocrisy. He always showed his blunt, rough side to the world, and his deeper nature only to his friends.

I never saw him alive, but I looked on his strong face with its massive crown of snow white hair as he lay in state in his casket in the Brick Church in New York City.

There are no tributes to his greatness on his tombstone, simply "Samuel Langhorne Clemens, Mark Twain. Nov. 30, 1835—April 21, 1910."

C.R. Taggart

Charlie Taggart loved his career, but especially his family and his home, Elmbank, in Newbury, Vermont. Writing to various Redpath officials, many of whom he had a personal friendship with, he often included a glimpse into his home life:

Charlie Taggart in his office at his Elmbank home, Newbury, Vermont, circa 1925. *From* Over the River and Through the Years *by Katharine Blaisdell, book six, 1984. Used by permission.*

June 4, 1914 [Newbury, Vermont]

Dear Mr. Crotty,-
...I have peas, lettuce, radishes, cress, beets, cucumbers, squashes and pumpkins all up and growing to beat the band! Fruit trees and ornamental shrubs just booming. My daughter came home from Northfield Seminary last night, so we are all together once more.

Cordially yours,
C.R. Taggart

Sept. 22nd, 1914 [Newbury, Vermont]

Dear Mr. McClure,
...I am enjoying my rest between Chautauqua and Lyceum work. I procured my hunters license the other day, and will spend some of the time in the woods.

My work begins Nov. 2nd in southern territory.

Mrs. Taggart and I will spend next Sunday with our two daughters who are in school at Northfield Seminary.

Cordially,
C.R. Taggart

Saybrook, Ill.
Dec. 12th, 1916

Dear Mr. Crotty,-
...I will be grateful if you can give me at least two weeks next year at Christmas, and I will find no fault if you give me the whole month of January as you did last year.

Cordially,
C.R. Taggart

Panora, Iowa,
Jan. 5th, 1917

Dear Mr. McClure,-
...I had a fine time at home for the Holidays. Went [caroling] *with the young folks Christmas morning...*

With best wishes,
[C.R. Taggart]

Stanford, Ky.
June 29th, 1921

Mr. Harry P. Harrison,
Chicago, Ill

Dear Mr. Harrison:-
...I have been trying to plan a little on next year...Miriam, my daughter in Smith College, graduates next June, and I am afraid it would break her heart if Dad and Mother were not there.

[C.R. Taggart]

Newbury, Vt.
Sept. 28th, 1921

Redpath Lyceum Bureau,
Chicago

Dear Mr. Crotty:-
...Have just [bought] *a Ford Sedan. Learning to run it.*

[C.R. Taggart]

October 6, 1921

Mr. C.R. Taggart,
Newbury, Vermont.

Dear Mr. Taggart:
...I certainly would like to see you spinning around in that Ford sedan.

[Crotty]

Newbury, Vt. Oct. 8th, 1921

Redpath Lyceum Bureau
Chicago

Dear Mr. Crotty:
... The Sedan works beautifully.

[C.R. Taggart]

Newbury, Vt.
Oct. 31, 1923

Mr. Ford Hicks
Redpath Lyceum Bureau
Chicago

Dear Mr. Hicks,
...O—I wonder if you have heard the news that I am called by neighbors ***Grandfather***—*James Hale Chamberlain was born Oct.*

2nd. My oldest daughter's son. Mother and baby here at home, and both doing fine.

Mr. Chamberlain [Taggart's son-in-law] *will come on bye and bye when James is strong enough, and take his family back to their home in Iowa.*

[C.R. Taggart]

Charlie Taggart and grandson Hale Chamberlain, circa 1924. *Courtesy of the Newbury, Vermont Historical Society.*

Charlie Taggart carrying grandson Hale Chamberlain, circa 1924. *Courtesy of the Newbury, Vermont Historical Society.*

Fairpoint, Iowa
Jan. 9th, 1926

Dear Mr. Harrison-
…All of our family were here but one daughter. I guess I told you that my daughter, Evelyn, has a very, very new and very charming granddaughter of mine. That makes two little folks that will call me Grandpa when they are older…

Cordially,
C.R. Taggart

Charlie Taggart behind his Elmbank home, circa 1925, "trying out a jig-tune."
From The Vermonter *magazine, November 1927.*

Newbury, Vt.
May 17th, 1926

Dear Mr. Harrison-
...Got my garden plowed today. Mrs. Taggart and Evelyn and her two children are coming Saturday from Iowa for the summer. We will be a united family again. It will be very nice to have a summer at home, but I can't afford another right away until Elisabeth is [through] *college.*

Best wishes to you and your family.

Cordially,
C.R. Taggart

American House, Boston, Mass.
Nov. 26th, 1927

Dear Mr. Harrison-
…No, the flood did not damage our property, but Mrs. Taggart and I were marooned for four days in our home. All exits with the car closed…

[C.R. Taggart]

Charlie Taggart had achieved success. He was able to give his three daughters something he never had: a college education. Evelyn graduated from the University of Missouri, while Miriam graduated from Smith College in Northampton, Massachusetts, where her mother, Edna, had attended. The youngest daughter, Elisabeth, graduated from Grinnell College in Iowa.

When he was home, Charlie had a "home orchestra" that periodically performed on the front porch of Elmbank and other venues locally in Newbury. The orchestra consisted of Charlie and his three daughters, with Evelyn on trumpet, Miriam playing the piano, Elisabeth on the violin and "Dad" Charlie on the slide trombone. Speaking of orchestras, it is said that John Philip Sousa visited Charlie and his family at Elmbank—but probably didn't join in with the "orchestra." These and many other family events at Elmbank were very dear in Charlie's memories.

Entertainment was changing in the 1920s. The public was drawn toward newer music and dance steps. Slapstick vaudeville comedy was increasingly popular. Radio and movies were becoming more common. The quaint fiddling, stories, impersonations and ventriloquism that Charlie Taggart had cultivated since 1895 were becoming passé, and it was getting harder for him to find work on the Redpath, which, itself, was going through a transformation. Charlie's routines were seen by many audiences as repetitive, even though he continued to develop more and more original material. In a letter to the Redpath, dated December 4, 1916, responding to complaints about his work, Charlie stated:

Every entertainer gives similar programs, because he is himself. It cannot be otherwise, and there always will be people who, when they have seen the same man, will think they have seen the same show. The reason people want me again is because they want more of the kind of work I do. The people as a whole usually like me better the second time than the first, and I do not believe the complaints are from honest spontaneous reasons.

View of the village of Newbury, Vermont, from Mount Pulaski in 2012, showing the Connecticut River and the mountains of New Hampshire in the background. Charlie Taggart recounts this view as one of the most beautiful in Vermont, and due to his love of hiking and mountain climbing, he was quite familiar with this vantage point. *Courtesy of Mary-Anne Boyce.*

In 1921, Charlie's low marks among audiences was concerning to the Redpath. Charlie responded in this letter to the Redpath main office in Chicago, dated June 7, 1921:

> *It is a surprise to hear that the reports on my work are not entirely satisfactory. Things have been going so well apparently, and Mr. Thomas's words of appreciation were so flattering, that side of the matter had not occurred to me. I am glad you told me. I will try and find the trouble and rectify it, if possible. We are never too old to learn. If you find on further investigation that the work I am doing is generally weak, and that I am not up to your standard, I will not beg for a moment to stay with you. I am convinced that Redpath standards are the highest, but I will not be out of work if I leave you.*

Apparently, officials at the Redpath were able to convince Charlie that they were generally pleased with his work, and he continued to be affiliated with them. However, Charlie appears to have had an accident, as the following letter from him to the Redpath indicates:

Clinton, Mich.
Aug. 31st, 1921

Mr. H.P. Harrison

Dear Mr. Harrison

...I will not be able to come to the I.L.C.A. convention this year. Possibly you know that I had a fall at No. Salem, Ind., and the doctors tell me that my knee should have absolute rest to [ensure] *having a perfect leg. That is impossible, but I must get where I can give it a good rest as soon as possible. I am somewhat awkward in my platform work, but the fiddle is O.K.,* [although] *it got soused in the water when I fell...*

Sincerely yours,
C.R. Taggart

Charlie also continued to push for a higher salary, as evidenced by the following exchange between him and the Redpath:

Newbury, Vt. Sept. 28th, 1921

Redpath Lyceum Bureau,
Chicago

Dear Mr. Crotty:-
Your letter received. Mr. Harrison told me that it was a mistake that my salary was not raised this year along with the rest, and that it would be raised next year. So, as he has not stated a price, I will do so. My terms will be $35.00 per day, take and leave at New York—time not to begin before Nov. 1st, and not to run later than March 1st. Three weeks at Christmas—winter contract only. I will make arrangements for Chautauquas separately. My present contract expires Apr. 1st, 1922.

Please let me hear from you at once. I would like a guarantee of ten weeks. I am having more independent calls for work here at home than I can take care of. All the men will just have to jump the selling price a little.

Cordially,
C.R. Taggart

October 6, 1921

Mr. C.R. Taggart,
Newbury, Vermont.

Dear Mr. Taggart:
Received your letter of recent date, and in reply wish to state that we are sending out a bulletin to the various offices who are planning on using you next year, and I am frank to tell you that I do not know what the come-back will be in regard to raising salaries.

It was the general [consensus] *of opinion that this is not the year to do anything of this type, even though some of the attractions should have been raised, like yourself. We are even asking some people to* [take] *a reduction—because—we positively cannot raise prices.*

Rest assured, Mr. Taggart, that we shall do whatever we can for you, as you have been more than good to us in every respect.

With kindest regards and best wishes, we are

Yours very truly,
THE REDPATH BUREAU
by
Mgr. Lyceum Dept.

Newbury, Vt. Oct. 8th, 1921

Redpath Lyceum Bureau
Chicago

Dear Mr. Crotty:
If my salary had been raised along with the rest last year, I would not have [thought] *of raising in this hard year.*

Now you see, I am not asking you to guarantee very much time. The Ohio office and the Chicago office are thrown out altogether this year.

> [Can't] *you use the time at a better price? I do not aim to be as high as the highest, but I think the quality of my work will deserve a fair selling price, don't you?... Tell me how much time you can guarantee at the new price, and I will stay with you. I need a good deal of time here in the east, for my independent dates. The Victor folks have booked me for two more records on my way, when I start west. Am busy preparing them...*

Ultimately, local managers weren't keen on booking Charlie at a higher salary. George S. Boyd, of the Redpath-Brockway Bureau of Pittsburgh, wrote the following to the Redpath main office in Chicago on October 14, 1921: "Count me out on Taggart at $35. per date. His kind of show isn't worth it."

Charlie Taggart was a fairly strong advocate for himself. He was always inquiring as to future bookings, and planning for other potential work in between Redpath commitments. In the following letter from the Redpath, dated March 19, 1925, Charlie got some bad news:

> *Dear Mr. Taggart:*
> *We have your letter in regard to next season, and am afraid we shall not be able to arrange very much time after the holidays for you next year, since most of the offices have completed a good share of their bookings.*
>
> *We will, however, do the best we can for you. We shall do our best to secure a few dates for you, but cannot promise anything definite. We explained this matter to you when you were here.*
>
> *Since there are not as many Chautauquas as there used to be, the managers are not making... combination Chautauqua and Lyceum contracts. It is almost impossible to do this, since the length of the circuits vary so much—some being seven weeks long and others about twenty weeks. Contracts are now made for the Lyceum season and Chautauqua season separately.*
>
> *Yours very truly,*
> *The Redpath Bureau*

To keep busy, Charlie was booking several independent dates in the Boston area. He also was booked with the Lincoln Chautauqua Bureau of Chicago, as well as the Swarthmore Chautauqua Bureau in Swarthmore, Pennsylvania. Undaunted, Charlie kept pushing the Redpath for potential dates:

Fairpoint, Iowa,
Jan. 19th, 1926

Dear Mr. Backman-
Anything in sight in the way of dates? I hope Morgan Park will reply soon, as I want to go east in March and April.

Concerning your letter of Jan. 8th- I am somewhat "up the stump" as they say, concerning next winter. As I wrote you, I have the fall up to Christmas with Swarthmore—after that, your agents are going to try and book some dates. I have had opportunities to sign up for definite time with others, but you have my circular plates—I have been with you fifteen years and more—to our mutual satisfaction and profit, I believe, and I like Redpath the best of them all. I really need to work more next winter than I am doing this. Is it absolutely too late for any definite contract for next winter? Of course, if there is a reasonable prospect of work, I would prefer to stay with you and take chances, than to go elsewhere.

Sorry to trouble you, but I am going to ask you to give me another statement of the definite offer you can give me for next winter.

Cordially,
C.R. Taggart

February 12, 1926
Mr. C.R. Taggart,
Fairpoint, Iowa

Dear Mr. Taggart:
. . . We are going ahead booking as many dates as we can on you. We have sent out several bulletins to the different offices, and hope they will sell a number of dates on you.

Drop in and see us on your way East.

Yours very truly,
THE REDPATH BUREAU
BY
C.E. BACKMAN

American House, Boston, Mass.
April 28th, 1926

Dear Mr. Backman-
...I can't see why your agents should have such a hard time selling "The Country Fiddler" this season at the regular price. Mr. White told me that my time is selling so well here largely on account of the fancy of Henry Ford in [bringing] *the Country Fiddlers into notice. My time is selling fine and all in the vicinity of Boston.* [Mr. White] *begged for a block of time to use in Lyceum in Ohio, but I cannot but give Redpath first choice as I have done for so long. So, if you are over stocked with talent and would prefer me to withdraw, please let me know definitely. If you do want me to remain, I hope you will not think it necessary to continue this emergency price longer than this season. But you know best what the men in my class are getting, and I do not want to be unreasonable.*

Best wishes,
C.R. Taggart

May 14, 1926

Mr. Chas. R. Taggart,
Newbury, Vermont

Dear Mr. Taggart:
The Chicago office is the only office that has booked any time on you. We have fifteen (15) dates booked.

[We] *note you are not quite satisfied with the agreement. We assure you these dates would not have been secured had we not booked you at a fee of $65.00* [a week]...

For some reason or other, entertainers are not very easy to sell in our territory, except at a low price. We hope conditions will improve in the course of a year or two.

Yours very truly,
THE REDPATH BUREAU
BY
C.E. BACKMAN

The summer of 1926 was the first summer since 1913 that Charlie Taggart had been without work. At age fifty-five, he still had one daughter, Elisabeth, in college, and needed to fund her remaining years of education. Charlie continued to fill dates wherever and whenever he could, always giving the Redpath first consideration. He continued entertaining in the Boston area, primarily for churches, banquets and local organizations—much the same sort of work he started doing for the Boston Lyceum Bureau and the Lovett Entertainment Bureau many years earlier.

"The Man from Vermont" would need to reinvent himself.

Hiawatha's Return from the Chautauquas
(C.R. Taggart, c. 1910)

Should you ask me for a letter
Telling of my journey westward,
Telling of my strange adventures,
On the road and in the country,
In the villages and wigwams,
On the broad and fertile prairies,
In the land of the Chautauquas:
I should answer, I should tell you
I am happy, O my brothers,
And my heart is light within me,
Like the eider-down my heart is.
For I'm speeding swiftly homeward
To my wigwam in the mountains,
To my people and my kindred
In the highlands of New England,
In the kingdom of the North-wind
In the regions of the morning.

Yet well spent has been the season,
Even tho' the sun above me
Glared upon me from the heavens;

The Man from Vermont

All the season glared upon me,
With his hot and burning visage,
Beating down upon the wigwams
Where the people were assembled
In the land of the Chautauquas.

Many days I've been among them,
On the road and in the country,
Passing in and out among them,
Cheering them with song and story,
Causing them to shout with laughter,
So that many spake on this wise,
"You have cheered us, O my brother,
And we're glad to have you with us;
Come again another season,
Come again and cheer our people.
Cheer our sons and cheer our daughters,
Cheer our young men and our old men,
With your songs and with your stories,
With your violin of hemlock."
Very pleasant are these greetings
From these people of the prairies
In the land of the Chautauquas.

No adventures have befallen
To detain me on my journey,
Nor to hinder me from keeping
All my various appointments,
And collecting all the wampum
For the mighty wampum keepers
In the kingdom of the bureaus,
In the land of cunning people,
In the kingdom of Chicago.

Chapter Seven

RE-INVENTING THE ACT, WITH SOME HELPING HANDS

Hold Your Horses
by Charles R. Taggart
*(*Lyceum Magazine, *December, 1915)*

Lyceum Workers, when you are jolted, yanked and bumped into a town on a freight train, and land in the mud with no rubbers; if you are in time for your work and if your health is good, don't fly all to pieces, but brush off the mud and be thankful that you have arrived.

HOLD YOUR HORSES!

If the committee does not meet you at the train, and nobody in sight knows of any hotel in town; don't vent your spleen upon the station agent. Wait till you hear the committee's side of the matter.

HOLD YOUR HORSES!

If you find there is no post office in Dinkeyville, but that mail for Dinkeyville all goes to Donkeyville, five miles away; don't go up in the air—the next man you meet may hand you a whole pocketful of letters.

HOLD YOUR HORSES!

If you are informed that you are to be entertained by Deacon Smith out in the country, don't wire to the county-seat for an auto to take you twenty-five miles after ten o'clock. You may find steam heat and an accessible bathroom and a hearty welcome by kind hearts to boot.

HOLD YOUR HORSES!

Part of a publicity brochure for a Chautauqua in Montpelier, Vermont, in 1927, featuring "Charles Ross Taggart and his Fiddlers." The additional two fiddlers was an attempt to bolster Taggart's bookings. *From left to right (upper panel):* Daniel Ross, Charlie Taggart and Harold Crosby. Crosby appears to have performed only in 1927, with Perley Klark of Woodsville, New Hampshire, taking his place for the final two tours of the troupe in 1928 and 1929. *Courtesy of the Redpath Chautauqua Bureau collection, University of Iowa Libraries, Iowa City.*

And most important of all: If the steam radiator pounds and a baby squalls, obliterating your climax, and people come in during your impressive passages; and if there has been neglect or mismanagement in any form on the part of the committee; keep steady. FIGHT IT OUT INSIDE. Don't show your weakness by yielding to the impulse to be sarcastic or to administer reproof to the audience. There's a reason. Show your poise and royalty of spirit by talking to apparent notice. Only amateurs undertake to reprove an audience from the platform. Smother your wrath and you will feel the joy of a conqueror by HOLDING YOUR HORSES!

In 1927, Crawford A. Peffer, eastern manager of the Redpath, suggested a change to Charlie Taggart's program: add two more fiddlers. Charlie had been a one-man act, and confidentially, he wasn't thrilled with the idea. However, over the course of time, he handpicked two very good fiddle players and one spare man.

Daniel Ross of Boston, Massachusetts, was a Scottish fiddler, actor and singer who had appeared in many local productions and sang twice a week for his church in Boston.

Perley Klark was from Woodsville, New Hampshire, northeasterly across the Connecticut River from Newbury village. Klark was the well-known head of Klark's Orchestra and was an excellent fiddler and piano player. As a matter of fact, Charlie's youngest daughter, Elisabeth, had taken lessons from Klark all during her time at Newbury High School.

The "spare man" was Harold Crosby, principal of the Newbury High School. According to Katharine Blaisdell's book *Over the River and Through the Years (Book Six)*, Crosby toured one season with Charlie and Dan Ross. This was actually a tryout of the new program, which included a Chautauqua in Montpelier, Vermont, in the summer of 1927. Charlie, in one letter to the Redpath, stated that Crosby wasn't as strong a player as Perley Klark, which probably explains why Crosby's name didn't appear on future itineraries.

The Redpath was delighted with the prospect, wanting the trio for both a Chautauqua, as well as a lyceum tour the next season, as the following letter indicated:

November 3, 1927

Mr. Charles R. Taggart,
Newbury, Vermont.

Dear Friend Taggart:
When Peffer was here he talked very enthusiastically about your Fiddlers' combination. I am wondering whether you would be interested in a Lyceum tour also with the same combination.

Our trouble here in building programs for our Chautauquas is to build better programs for less money. Our single admissions have dropped off frightfully the last two years. Our season ticket sales have had a slight increase, which, of course, is good for the permanency of the Chautauqua, but it will be necessary for us to re-adjust our contract for the sale of season tickets before we can reap any benefits from that source.

If you would be willing to take $150.00 a week and... two good fiddlers for $50.00 [each] *a week, so that the company would not cost us over $250.00, I feel sure we could use a good Lyceum season as well as* [a] *Chautauqua.*

We are having our meeting here the latter part of next week or the early part of the week following, and we should have to know definitely before that meeting.

Sincerely yours,
Harry P. Harrison

The trio went by several names: Taggart and His Fiddlers, Charles Ross Taggart and His Old-Time Country Fiddlers and The Old Country Fiddler and His Fiddlers' Three. It was billed as entertainment "entirely unique" and "not like any you ever attended." A publicity brochure for the trio gave kudos to Charlie Taggart as being "known the country over" through his recordings and Phonofilm appearance, adding, "No Lyceum or Chautauqua entertainer has gained greater fame."

Charlie, while staying in Boston in December 1927, acknowledged receipt of the contract for the trio in the following letter to Harry Harrison of the Redpath:

American House, Boston, Mass.
Dec. 2nd, 1927

Dear Mr. Harrison-

Contracts here O.K. Mr. Klark is coming Monday morning for the pictures, and I will forward the contract, signed by the three of us, as you have made it all into one. I am no lawyer, but it looks all right... We are all very enthusiastic over the prospect. Like ten year old boys. Mr. Klark is planning to get a new closed car for the trip, and will drive the three of [us], *if it will be possible. He will be anxious to hear about this, as he would like*

A publicity brochure featuring Charles Ross Taggart and His Old Time Country Fiddlers, circa 1928. *Courtesy of the Newbury, Vermont Historical Society.*

Inside of a 1928 brochure for Charles Ross Taggart and His Old Time Country Fiddlers. *From left to right:* Daniel Ross, Charles Ross Taggart and Perley Klark. *Courtesy of the Newbury, Vermont Historical Society.*

to change his car for a closed one very soon, as he can get a better trade, I suppose. It will also be interesting to know which circuit we will be on.

Cordially,
C.R. Taggart

Charlie Taggart and his "Fiddlers' Three" officially started in Waycross, Georgia, on April 24, 1928. The four-month Chautauqua tour went throughout the South and Midwest, including Florida, South Carolina, North Carolina, Tennessee, Alabama, Kentucky, Illinois, Indiana, Michigan and Wisconsin, ending on August 16.

The trio would entertain again in early 1929 on a lyceum tour, starting on January 7 in Utica, New York, and going on to Ohio, West Virginia, Kentucky, Indiana, Illinois, Iowa, Minnesota, Michigan and Virginia, ending in Shickshinny, Pennsylvania, on April 13. There are no known reviews

Publicity shot for Charles Ross Taggart and His Old Time Fiddlers, 1928. *From left to right:* Daniel Ross, Charles Ross Taggart and Perley Klark. *Courtesy of the Newbury, Vermont Historical Society.*

of either of these tours, but it is presumed that they were well received. It wasn't quite enough, however, to sway the tide of a fast-changing culture of audiences. There would be no further tours for the trio.

In between these "Fiddlers' Three" tours, Charlie convinced the Redpath to put him and his youngest daughter, Elisabeth, on a Chautauqua tour together. Unlike her older sisters, who both attended Northfield Seminary in Massachusetts, Elisabeth Taggart was a graduate of Newbury High School, class of 1924. She had been a co-editor of the school newspaper, the *Live Wire*, but also enjoyed music. She attended Grinnell College in Iowa, graduating in 1928 with a degree in music.

Charlie and Elisabeth were booked on a Chautauqua tour in the Rochester, New York area, starting on September 21, 1928, in Stockton and ending on December 13 in Otto. Charlie, in his unpublished *Vermont Life* article, remembered the tour, saying, "We arranged a little dialogue sketch, and with our two violins we varied the program, with pleasure for us, and apparently for our audiences."

In Prospect, New York, on November 22, 1928, Elisabeth wrote her perspective about the same tour, which appeared in the *Live Wire* in Newbury:

Charlie Taggart and daughter Elisabeth in a publicity photo for their 1928 Chautauqua season in western New York state. *From* Over the River and Through the Years *by Katharine Blaisdell, book six, 1984. Used by permission.*

> *My father and I are on one of the Redpath Festival circuits, which is really a sort of indoor Chautauqua. This circuit is managed by the Rochester office of the Redpath bureau, and is entirely in New York State. There are four numbers on the course, coming just a week apart. We, being the second company, follow the first company, coming to the towns…just a week behind them. The first and last…are concert companies, giving musical programs entirely; the third is a lecturer on Abraham Lincoln, who also impersonates*

Lincoln, and our program is a combination of music and fun. Of course, it is all a new experience for me, but a very interesting and enjoyable one, in spite of some difficulties.

We are entertained, as a rule, in private homes, although, in some places, we are sent to hotels—if the town affords one! We find all sorts of homes, good, bad and indifferent, although we have been fortunate for the most part. Sometimes we go from one extreme to the other, as we did two weeks ago. On Friday, we were entertained in an [exceptionally] *nice home—lovely people, and all* [the] *conveniences. Then the next day, we found a place that we will remember forever as one to keep away from! We had a drive of 84 miles to begin with, and reached the town about half past twelve* [p.m.]. *Our usual plan is to go to the Post Office first, to get our mail and find out where we are to stay. Here, however, we discovered that the Post Office was closed during the noon hour, so we had to go elsewhere for information. We asked the storekeeper, but he knew nothing about it; neither could the minister tell us anything. Finally, we were obliged to drive half a mile up a steep, muddy hill to the home of the chairman of the committee, only to learn that our abiding place was three miles back, over the same road by which we had come! There was nothing to do but go back...so back we went, though inwardly rebellious. We were still more rebellious when we arrived to find cold rooms, with not even curtains at the windows, no electricity or gas, no bathroom, and things not too clean. A pleasant prospect over Sunday! We usually stay in our Saturday town over Sunday and play in church, but we just couldn't face it there, especially as we were both very much "under the weather" with colds and* [headaches].

We packed up Sunday morning and struck out for the nearest city and a warm hotel, where we could be comfortable. Such experiences are few and far between, however. We have had but one other such place, at the very beginning of the circuit. There we had to put the car in the hen-house! You can imagine the rest of the surroundings for yourselves!

We are driving our own car, which makes the trip much more pleasant and convenient than it would be by train. We can take as much baggage as we please—at least as much as the back seat of our Ford Sedan will hold—and can go and come when it suits us. We have taken several interesting side trips from some of our towns. One day we drove to Letchworth Park, a state park on the Genesee River. There are three lovely falls and several spots of historical interest. The whole Genesee country is interesting, from a historical standpoint. We visited the place which marked the end of the Revolution, in Cuylerville, and several

Elisabeth Taggart beside Charlie Taggart's 1921 Ford Model T Sedan, which they used on their 1928 Chautauqua tour in New York state. *Courtesy of the Newbury, Vermont Historical Society.*

places connected [with] *the early Indian wars. Twice we have driven into Rochester for a little recreation. The new Eastman Theater there is very lovely…* [Election Day] *we spent in Geneva. Needless to say, there was great excitement, especially from seven o'clock* [p.m.] *on. Bulletins were flashed on an outdoor screen, and crowds of people were gathered on the sidewalks all evening. Such cheering when news came that New York State had gone for* [Herbert] *Hoover instead of its own Governor* [Al] *Smith.*

We have been very fortunate with regard to weather and car trouble so far. We drove over 500 miles from Newbury to our first date, which was in the very western part of New York, with no tire or engine trouble at all, and have had no trouble on the road since then. Three punctures (with garages conveniently near), a broken connection on our starter, and [a] *broken door lock are the extent of our difficulties. We had snow for the first time yesterday, except one or two little flurries a few weeks ago. We are just now getting down out of the "North Country," so we are not surprised at the snow. We were up near Ogdensburg, on the St. Lawrence River last weekend—our "dash to the pole" we call it, as we had only three dates in that region, and made a long jump to get there, and another to get back.*

After the New York Chautauqua tour with Elisabeth, Taggart went back to Newbury to get ready for his second and final tour with the "Fiddlers' Three" in early 1929. In 1930, he wrote to see if the Redpath had any future bookings planned for him and Elisabeth. The following letter answered Charlie's question:

April 21, 1930

Mr. C.R. Taggart,
Newbury, Vermont.

Dear Friend Taggart:
I have just talked with Mr. Backman, and he seems to think it would be very unwise, both for us, as well as for you and [Elisabeth], *to attempt a season this coming year.*

As you doubtless know, all the entertainment field has taken a very peculiar turn, and no one knows just where [it] *is at present, and, if you can get any definite work for this coming season anywhere, and want it, I certainly would take it.*

With all good wishes,
Sincerely yours,
[Harry Harrison]

Charlie was now almost sixty years old, and the prospects were far from encouraging. An entire lifetime of work was behind him, and the Great Depression stared straight ahead. What would the future hold for Charlie Taggart? Were his best days behind him?

Chapter 8

THE FINAL BOW

Reflectors
by C.R. Taggart
*(*Lyceum Magazine, *undated)*

I wonder how many of us platformists realize that we are, or should be, Reflectors. Reflectors of beauty in its various forms-the beauty of language, which is literature; the beauty of tone and tones, and their combinations, which is music. I should not assume the attitude of a big Ego, or something in a dress-suit to be looked at, and listened to, and admired, and applauded, but I should be a clear Reflector of things that are worth while [sic].

If I have the power to discern humor in things and situations, and reflect them with a decisive flash in gesture or word to a crowd of miscellaneous people, that is my valuable gift that I should be proud to use. If I can see and feel beauty in the literature of the great masters, and can reflect it, I am rendering a service that way. Also, if I have the skill to produce with finger or voice the beauty in harmonies, what a pleasant and profitable performance it should be to reflect it to my audience!

The idea is not original to me. I got it from Henry Drummond's little book, "The Greatest Thing in the World." The definite idea he presents is that according to the suggestion from the New Testament, we should reflect the spirit of the Christ.

As it seems to me this morning, good lyceum friends, this is a vital part of our service to the world, to be Reflectors.

This circa 1935 photo shows Charlie Taggart at Elmbank with (left to right, back) daughter Elisabeth, wife Edna and daughters Miriam and Evelyn. Granddaughter Elinor, daughter of Evelyn, is in front. *Courtesy of Ross Chamberlain.*

By 1932, the Redpath Lyceum and Chautauqua Bureau, which Charlie Taggart had faithfully served for so many years, had given its last program. American entertainment had changed, especially with the advent of radio and talking movies. Charlie managed to get affiliated with the Alkahest Celebrity Bureau of Atlanta, Georgia, for his "winter season," getting as far south as Florida. He also booked a number of independent gigs, but it was far from his highpoint in the Redpath years. Many of these bookings were very similar to the way he started out in the late 1890s—on a profit-sharing plan— getting half or two-thirds of the admission price. In Orlando, Florida, on March 14, 1935, he gave a program at the Central Christian Church, receiving the grand total of $3.50, which was half of the collection. This was far from Charlie's usual salary of $25.00 with the Redpath, but even less than his very first performance in 1895, where he received $7.50, after expenses. His average salary in this time period was about $15.00.

Charlie drove to most of these programs in the 1930s. By this time, he had probably traded in the old Model T Ford Sedan for the Model A he nicknamed "Danny." From Florida, in January 1935, he headed north, working his way up the East Coast, arriving in New England by early May, in time to appear in various and sundry local events—primarily schools, churches, fraternal organizations and banquets. Some of his engagements that year included High Point College in North Carolina; Tennessee Polytechnic Institute in Cookeville; the Tremont Temple Sunday School Banquet in Boston; Riverside Military Academy in Gainsville, Georgia; Kimball Union Academy in Meriden, New Hampshire; the Vermont Rural Mail Carriers Banquet in Windsor; the Beverly, Massachusetts Woman's Club; the Congregational Church in Saxtons River, Vermont; and the Acton, Massachusetts Town Hall, for the Juvenile Grange—a grand total of forty appearances for the entire year of 1935.

In 1936, Charlie managed to get fifty-nine appearances, only getting as far south as Cranford, New Jersey. The majority were in New York State and New England. On February 9, he was featured on a radio broadcast on WABC in New York.

On January 21, 1937, Charlie Taggart was back in the south, at the Orlando, Florida Sanitarium, the first of nine scheduled appearances for that year. He was in Bradenton, Florida, on February 8—two programs on the same day, number eight and nine on his schedule—first, for the local Rotary luncheon and then later at the Tourist Club. At this point in his handwritten itinerary, found in an old ledger book, his performances abruptly end, skipping to May 12, 1939. According to the Newbury, Vermont Historical Society and other local sources, Charlie Taggart, while giving a performance in 1937, suffered a stroke.

Based on his antics of the past, including various tricks and impersonations, his audience thought the stroke was simply part of the act. Unfortunately, the affliction was quite real. Charlie suffered "partial paralysis in the lips and one hand," and his "versatility was somewhat curtailed," according to Book Six of Katharine Blaisdell's series *Over the River and Through the Years*. Undaunted, Charlie reworked his program to include one-handed piano pieces with his left hand, and for his trademark instrument, the fiddle, he strapped the fiddle bow onto his paralyzed right hand with a loose rubber band.

It is not known how many performances Charlie gave between February 8, 1937, and May 12, 1939. On the latter date, he appeared in Providence, Rhode Island, for the local Camp Fire Girls at Trinity Methodist Episcopal Church.

The decision was made by Charlie Taggart to retire, which, again, according to local sources, was in 1938. We don't know if this was a voluntary decision, or whether there were other factors. It had been Charlie's only occupation for forty-three years. Edna Taggart, Charlie's wife, was severely afflicted with

Charlie Taggart and grandson Ross, circa 1942.
Courtesy of Ross Chamberlain.

arthritis, which may have been another contributing reason for his retirement from entertaining. Charlie and Edna left their beloved Elmbank in Newbury, Vermont, to live with their eldest daughter, Evelyn, and her family in Brevard, North Carolina. Elmbank continued to be used as a summer retreat for some of the Taggart daughters and their friends, until it was finally sold in 1947.

Charlie Taggart still did occasional programs during the remainder of his life in the various places where his daughter's family lived. He did a total of fourteen appearances from 1940 to 1952, most of them free of charge, with an occasional free meal included.

Charlie and Edna's son-in-law, Thomas Chamberlain, was a fisheries biologist who traveled all over the United States, stocking trout ponds for the Fish and Wildlife Service. So began another tour, if you will, for "The Man from Vermont." The family, consisting of Charlie and Edna, daughter Evelyn, son-in-law Thomas and youngest grandson and Charlie's namesake, Charles Ross Chamberlain, relocated from Brevard, North Carolina, to San Carlos, Arizona, circa 1943. For a short time, Charlie's other two Chamberlain grandchildren, Hale and Elinor, were also with them until Hale went into the U.S. Army, and Elinor went to nurses' training. Charlie's itinerary ledger mentioned a program he gave in San Carlos on May 2, 1944, confirming the time period they lived there.

By 1946, the family was living in College Station, Texas. It was during this time that Charlie was compiling an article about his life's career as a musical humorist for the newly created *Vermont Life* magazine. In the first paragraph, Charlie wrote:

The Taggarts and their grandchildren in College Station, Texas, circa 1946. *From top left and down:* Hale (on porch), Elinor and Ross. *Courtesy of Doris McClintock.*

Charlie Taggart in College Station, Texas with (left to right) daughters Miriam and Evelyn and grandson Ross, circa 1947. *Courtesy of Doris McClintock.*

> *When I write a letter to a person, that person is always in mind as I write. In my travel letters to the home paper (The* United Opinion, *Bradford, Vt.), I always felt as tho' the readers of the paper were my addressees. Now, as VERMONT LIFE is having such a wide circulation, I must address not only Vermonters, but outsiders as well. I have many friends in Vermont who know all about me, but for others, these items of my career may be of interest.*

For unknown reasons, the article was rejected by *Vermont Life*.

While in College Station, Edna Taggart's health continued to decline. Using crutches in the early 1940s, her arthritis kept getting more severe, until she was wheelchair bound, and by the late 1940s, she remained in her bed as an invalid. Edna died in College Station on May 3, 1950.

The family stayed in College Station for another two years. For Charlie's sake, the family decided to relocate in mid-1952 to Readfield (pronounced Reedfield), Maine, approximately twelve miles northwest of the state capital at Augusta, in the locality known as Kents Hill. It was here that young grandson Ross was to attend the Kents Hill Academy, and Charlie could once again be in New England, his original home region.

Before leaving College Station, Charlie gave his last two performances, according to his ledger, both in 1952: April 15 in Bryan, and April 21 in College Station—both for the local Lions' clubs. He hadn't given a program since 1947 but was able to rise to the occasion, as the retired professional entertainer he was. Charlie's April 21 program, which he noted "same as Apr. 15," included a myriad of his famous birdcalls, stories and fiddle tunes, including *Haste to the Wedding*, *Flowers of Edinburgh*, *Pig Town Fling*, *Devil's Dream* and *Money Musk*.

By the summer of 1952, Charlie, his daughter Evelyn and his son-in-law Thomas were in Lebanon, New Hampshire, staying with friends. In the late summer, grandson Ross, who had spent part of the summer at a YMCA camp in South Carolina, traveled by bus to White River Junction, Vermont, and joined the family at Lebanon. Together, they visited with friends of Charlie and Evelyn and toured various sites around the area, including Elmbank in Newbury, and Charlie's original stomping grounds in East Topsham. It also appears that Charlie Taggart visited his alma mater, the Mount Hermon School in Northfield, Massachusetts, that same summer. It would be the last time that he would ever see any of these familiar old sites again.

By September 1952, the family was residing in Readfield, Maine, at Kents Hill, in a house directly across from the Kents Hill Academy, where Charlie's grandson, Ross, was attending. It was the beginning of the last ten months of

Charlie Taggart's life. The fiddle tunes, stories and various impersonations and tricks that he had accumulated over a lifetime were fading away. On January 20, 1953, Charlie's left leg was amputated above the knee, which, for a man who walked and climbed mountains in his younger years, must have been quite demoralizing (Charlie wrote that the amputation actually took place on February 12, but his physician stated January 20). Nonetheless, he wrote the following on a plain white postcard to Mr. Lester P. White of the Mount Hermon School, dated March 20, 1953:

> *Dear Mr. White,*
> *I'm recovering from a leg amputation... What a pleasant meeting we had last summer...My left leg is off above the knee. Evelyn sends greetings to you and Mrs. W.*
>
> *Charles Ross Taggart*

Written in pencil on the front of the same postcard, by someone at Mount Hermon, was the following, which probably appeared in an upcoming school newsletter: "Following amputation of his left leg above the knee, Charles R. Taggart reports a good recovery. He is 82 now, and lives at Kents Hill, Maine."

Charles Ross Taggart, "The Man from Vermont," died on July 4, 1953, at Kents Hill. An obituary, which appeared in the *Barre* (Vermont) *Daily Times* on July 8 of that year, said of Taggart, "To the end, Mr. Taggart maintained vigor of mind, a cheerful spirit, and his unfailing sense of humor. He spent much time happily corresponding with his wide circle of friends."

Charlie Taggart was laid to rest in the Readfield Corner Cemetery, with only a plain, flush grass marker of granite, displaying just his name and the years of his existence.

Over a half century earlier, in December 1901, while Charlie Taggart was in Concord, Massachusetts, he visited the famous Sleepy Hollow Cemetery, where he saw the graves of literary giants such as Nathaniel Hawthorne, Ralph Waldo Emerson and Louisa May Alcott. He noted that, although they were great writers, they had very simple gravestones. Charlie wrote, "I learned this lesson from my visit to Sleepy Hollow Cemetery: that true greatness does not require great tombstones to perpetuate memory."

Charlie Taggart, in the late 1940s, wrote the following about his life and career: "My life has been a pleasant one. I always wanted to travel and got plenty of that. I always loved to make folks laugh, and that wish was satisfied."

From an early publicity sheet of his, during the Redpath years, Charlie summed up what was his life's work by saying, "If I can turn your pain into

The gravestone of Charles Ross Taggart at the Readfield Corner Cemetery in Readfield, Maine. *Courtesy of Mary-Anne Boyce.*

pleasure by music, your worries into wonderment by mimicry, and your sadness to smiles by humor—in short, if I can succeed in lifting the cares and burdens from your life, for one evening only, my purpose will have been accomplished."

In 1927, he was asked by interviewer Lois Goodwin Greer of the *Vermonter* magazine if he would ever write a book about his experiences, to which Charlie replied:

> *Well, now, in my opinion, a book has to have some justification for being, before it can lay claim to any amount of circulation. I suppose you think I might privately publish these "experiences"...but I have noticed that nearly all books thus published are usually more or less of a failure, especially from a commercial standpoint...I'd better stick to my fiddle, to my impersonations and monologues; perhaps this way I can scatter a little sunshine, and make the world a little easier to live with by giving it a good laugh now and again.*

Perhaps Lois Goodwin Greer wrote the most apt description of the life of Charles Ross Taggart, and his contributions to our cultural heritage, from that same interview, twenty-six years before his death:

> *It was not Henry Ford who* [re]*introduced the old jig and hornpipe tunes to America. Charles Ross Taggart had been fiddling and singing his way into the hearts of his countrymen for a quarter century before Mr. Ford's belated interest in these tingling melodies...* [Charles Ross Taggart] *has fiddled and talked himself into the lives of the men, women and children of these great United States in town and city and country, leaving each one a little cheered, a little happier for his passing.*

FINIS

POSTSCRIPT

On October 8, 2011, Vermont governor Peter Shumlin issued a proclamation for "Charles Ross Taggart Day" in the state of Vermont.

On that same day, two markers were dedicated to honor "The Old Country Fiddler." The first one, a bronze plaque, donated by Adam and Mary-Anne Boyce, was placed on the front of the Topsham Town Hall in East Topsham village, where exactly 116 years earlier, Charles Ross Taggart had launched his career as a traveling entertainer by giving his first public performance in that very hall.

Later that day, a Vermont Historic Roadside Marker, furnished by the Vermont Division for Historic Preservation, through the efforts of the Newbury Historical Society, was placed in front of Taggart's former home, Elmbank, in Newbury, on U.S. Route 5.

Postscript

State of Vermont
Executive Department
A Proclamation

WHEREAS, Charles Ross Taggart was born in 1871 and grew up in Topsham before living in Newbury for many years; and

WHEREAS, as a jack of all trades, Taggart farmed, taught school, and repaired watches before becoming a professional entertainer in the mid 1890s;

WHEREAS, with famous characters known as "the Old Country Fiddler" and "the Man from Vermont," Taggart was a musical humorist, traveling all over the United States in various Lyceum and Chautauqua tours, and eventually becoming a mainstay with the world famous Redpath Bureau of Chicago; and

WHEREAS, in 1923, Taggart became one of the first talking motion picture stars, appearing in a phono-film created by his former classmate, Dr. Lee de Forest; and

WHEREAS, throughout his illustrious career, Taggart produced over 40 recordings on labels such as Victor, Edison, and Columbia; and

WHEREAS, in 1938, Taggart retired from the entertainment industry, one year after suffering a stroke on stage; and

WHEREAS, in 1953, Taggart died in Kents Hill, Maine;

NOW, THEREFORE, I, Peter Shumlin, Governor, do hereby proclaim October 8, 2011 as

CHARLES ROSS TAGGART DAY

in Vermont and recognize Mr. Taggart for his contributions to the Green Mountain State.

Given under my hand and the Great Seal of the State of Vermont this 26 day of September, A.D. 2011.

Peter Shumlin
Governor

Left: Proclamation of Charles Ross Taggart Day by Governor Peter Shumlin on October 8, 2011. *Courtesy Adam R. Boyce.*

Below: The Topsham Town Hall, where Charlie Taggart debuted as an entertainer on October 8, 1895. Taken on Charles Ross Taggart Day, October 8, 2011. *Courtesy of Mary-Anne Boyce.*

Plaque on the front of the Topsham Town Hall in East Topsham, Vermont, which was dedicated on Charles Ross Taggart Day, October 8, 2011. *Courtesy of Mary-Anne Boyce.*

Author Adam Boyce (left) with Bill Hodge, president of the Topsham Historical Society, in front of the Topsham Town Hall, at the unveiling of the plaque honoring Charlie Taggart on Charles Ross Taggart Day, October 8, 2011. *Courtesy Mary-Anne Boyce.*

Above: This Vermont roadside historical marker to Charles Ross Taggart stands in front of his former Newbury home, Elmbank, along U.S. Route 5, just north of Newbury village. The marker was applied for by the Newbury Historical Society and furnished by the Vermont Division for Historic Preservation. It was unveiled on Charles Ross Taggart Day, October 8, 2011. *Courtesy of Mary-Anne Boyce.*

Left: Those in attendance at the Newbury festivities on Charles Ross Taggart Day on October 8, 2011. *Courtesy of Mary-Anne Boyce.*

Appendix A

SELECTED LETTERS OF CHARLES ROSS TAGGART

Marlborough, MA
April 29, 1905

Editor, United Opinion:

Yesterday in company with a friend, I spent the greater part of the day in visiting some of the points of historical interest in old Concord, Mass. It was my second visit and my friend's first and our enjoyment was so great that I wondered if some of your readers would not like to follow us on our rambles.

Anyway, here goes.

After leaving the train, we directed our steps first to the old Wright's Tavern, built in 1747, which was the headquarters of the Minute men (*sic*), where in case of an alarm being given of the approach of the British soldiers, they were to repair immediately for orders, and which was later used by the British as their headquarters, but not for long. The rooms are in their original condition, excepting furniture. Across one corner of the old office now used as a dining room, the same bar stands over which Maj. Pitcairn stirred his brandy and made his boast that he would "stir the blood of the d—d rebels before night."

Next we bent our footsteps towards the old north bridge and the battle ground, and the "Old Manse." These were seen under much more favorable conditions than formerly, as then the snow was just melting and the roads and fields lacked the beauty they now presented. Young leaves just starting, grass green and fresh, and sky blue. We did not spend much time dreaming of the past, as my friend had his camera and both our minds were occupied with the delightful task of getting some good pictures. After a light lunch at a clean little bakery restaurant and another picture of Wright's Tavern and Concord square, we shed all superfluous luggage and started with a swinging gait for Walden Woods, bent on finding Thoreau's hut and gazing upon the scenes once familiar to that great philosopher who preferred the society of woods and woodchucks to that of his fellow men.

We inquired of nearly ever[y] person we met who looked like a probable resident of the town the way to Thoreau's hut and were given so many confusing directions that we could only choose among them all the one(s) that seemed to us the most reasonable. The distance we were told was a mile and a half. On the way, we had a fine view of the rear of Ralph Waldo Emerson['s] house and we could also see the woods on the Hawthorne premises, but not the house. But the road soon led us away from the town into the woods and to Walden Pond, where we [began] our search for the famous hut which one man told us was on the shore of the pond, and another that it was on the top of a hill. We tramped around all the possible sites on both shore and hill, becoming more and more heated in body, and more and more determined in mind to discover the object of our search. My friend at last came to the conclusion in his own mind that the hut had been destroyed, but I wished to look at one place we had missed, so I did, and found a place were there were unmistakable signs of something made of old boards, having been demolished and some of the boards taken for a raft which was moored close by. So here thought I is the spot where the lonely hermit dwelt; that little clearing was probably his garden. I saw a broken chair half covered with leaves, which I reasoned was doubtless one in which the great naturalist had often set, and perhaps written in his journal, so I broke off a leg and wiped the dirt from it and rejoiced in being able to secure such a prize. There was the lake in which he sat in his boat and thought those wonderful thoughts which then or later got into his journal. Here, too, in winter, he chased a fox on the ice and his friend, the woodchuck, might have dwelt in yonder bank. Perhaps this was the very pine tree he compared to an Indian warrior. But my reverie was broken by the shouts of my companion, who had tired of waiting and coming after me. But ah! What a dissipation of all my fine dreams came when I returned to Wright's Tavern and inquired of the proprietor if the hut had been visited this year. "No," he replied. I said, "what a horrid shame it was for those wanderers, who ever they were, to tear it down to get material for a raft." He said, "I'm sorry to say, my friend, that it was used for a much meaner purpose. Several years ago, it was taken away whole and used for a hen house." "But," I said, "there was certainly something destroyed there." "O[h] yes," he said, "that was used for a picnic ground for several years and no doubt what you saw was some of the remnants of the old seats or tables." My cherished chair leg depreciated in value about two hundred per cent [*sic*].

"But where was the cabin," I said. "A pile of stones marks the spot," said he. A "cairn" they called it. Now I had noticed that pile of stones and wondered what it signified, if anything. I thought possibly it might be the result of some of Thoreau's agricultural efforts.

Well, well, so I dreamed in the wrong place. Never mind. I'll go back some day and dream at the real site by the cairn. Anyway, we saw the pond and had a good time chasing around, and my dream did me just as much good as if my pine tree and garden spot and woodchuck hole had been the real ones.

How good it felt to sit down in the cool railroad station with our dusty shoes and wilted collars, and to look at our souvenir cards and my chair leg. I shall still preserve it as a memento of the day.

C.R. Taggart

Trip to Moosilauke
(June 23, 1906)

Editor, United Opinion,

It was suggested that I tell our readers a little about our Moosilauke trip so I will review it on paper with them.

Twenty-four of us went, all the way to the top and back again, rain or shine, and enjoyed it, or appeared to. We had planned to go and although the weather wouldn't come out square and say Friday night what it was going to be Saturday, although it hinted "rain" and its mouthpiece, the weather bureau man, said "rain"; still the majority said "go." So we went, three-two horse teams of us, eight seats, three on a seat, fifteen boys and nine girls. These boys and girls consisted respectively of one minister, two teachers, thirteen scholars and eight miscellaneous people. Some of us were quite young and others still younger.

The band wagon went ahead, also the choir. These two organizations rendered selections appropriate to the occasion free of charge.

We started at 5:30 AM and arrived at the foot of the Glen Cliff Trail, stabled the horses, and were all ready to begin climbing at 8:45. The weather had made various promises all the way and as patches of blue sky were visible, we started full of hope for a good view from the top.

Now, people, if you have never climbed a Mountain, you can't imagine the rest. I suppose the very fact of our all aiming for the same thing in the same way and sharing joys and discomforts with a common hope, gave us a general spirit of comradeship and interest in each other and caused our good cheer to burst forth in laughter, shouts, and heartfelt expressions of admiration for all the beauties of the way.

Just come with me for a little as we go up.

"Hello! Everybody!" shouts our leader, who is the soul of the party. "Keep together as much as possible!" But we didn't. Some couldn't restrain their eagerness to reach the top and so skipped along ahead. On, on, we go, up the road, under the bars, through the pasture, into the wood. Now comes the long vista of tall spruces. What shall we call it? "Cathedral Aisle"? The spring where we drink from the varied assortment of drinking cups from the wine glass to the "hot water bag." Up, up, up! On the logs! The trail winding around in beautiful curves. New beauties at every step. Alpine stocks are whittled out from saplings.

Whew! Let's stop and rest.

"O[h] dear! Are we 'most there?"

"O[h], ho, ho! 'Most there!"

"Say folks, he wants to know if we are 'most there!"

"Just got well started, my boy."

Up, up, up. Now we come to the region of huge rocks with dark caves under them.

"Bears around here most likely."

"Ooo, don't let's talk about it."

"I'd like to see one."

"Well, you won't, not with this crowd around."

Now acres and acres of moss, and beautiful vegetation. Up, up, up. Now the trees are short and scrubby, and the trail grows steeper, and more rocky.

But I must pass over many, many interesting incidents: the lunch party, the tomb, the Newbury memorial column, the rain, the big sea of blue sky at which we all gave three cheers, the lost sweater, the hat that blew away and was never found. On, on, and up, up, until, at last—

Appendix A

"Hurrah!"

"The road!"

"Civilization at last!"

"And a telephone wire. Think of it!"

"How high did you say the mountain is?"

"4,810 ft."

"My! Ain't we up though."

The view was not quite as extensive as we had anticipated. However, the cloud effect was very pronounced. Sort of a sameness to the coloring, but the general effect was very striking. Some of us were so overcome by it that we could hardly stand; but we finally conquered our emotions and bent our steps towards the house. The cloud effect seemed intensified as we neared the house, and it made such an impression on us that we couldn't get rid of it even after we had gained that shelter, but the wonderful impressions the cloud made upon us dripped from the ends of our noses and from the tips of our ears and steamed from our coats and sweaters and skirts and trousers as we sat by the fire.

But we were a happy crowd. Most of us looked as though we had been doused in a rain water barrel by the heels, but what of that! We cared more about how we felt than how we looked, and most of us felt like coffee. So we all had some coffee, and looked at each other and laughed and said, fifty times a-piece, how we wouldn't have missed it for anything in the world. We told conundrums and whittled our alpinstocks (we boys; the girls were all out in the kitchen in various conditions of recuperations and reconstruction). Our good host and hostess were very kind and did everything they could for our comfort and cheered us by telling us what a lovely view they had about nine o'clock in the morning.

We arrived, I mean the tail end of the party, at the Tip Top House at 12:30, and left at 2:40 pm, reaching the teams at 4:45. We would have made quite a picture as we left the house, with handkerchiefs tied over our heads to keep the cloud out of our ears, racing at the top of our speed for the shelter of the woods.

O[h], I presume "all the leaves on all the trees" laughed at us as our little feetlets went pattering down over the rocks, and perhaps they said as our land-lady did, "Didn't you know this morning it was going to rain?" What cared we? To be sure, the rain was now sprinkling the trees and greasing the slippery logs and stones, and making our trail wet and muddy. But the wetter we got, the happier we were, apparently. And some got partially dry while the teams were being hitched up and we started home with a song and shout.

Appendix A

It just poured most of the way home, so our gladness soon knew no bounds, and we sang and tooted and shouted and yelled, and "woke 'em up" all along the way home; didn't we, folks?

What if some of us did sit in little pools of rain water most of the way home and what if some of us did get umbrella drippings down our backs and umbrella tips in our ears! And what if the eave spouts were directly over our laps and what if some of us couldn't get our shoes on again after we had taken them off to warm our feet! All these things didn't count.

The best side of all of us kept coming out all the way up and down and home, in such deeds of helpfulness, such words of good cheer, such determined grasping of all the beauties at hand, and such determined rejecting of all unpleasantnesses, that we all became better acquainted with the good side of each other. And also, we were greatly encouraged in this by the man who planned the trip…I mean, the man who disguised himself so thoroughly that our good landlady didn't suspect him of being a minister, but allowed her suspicions to rest on an entirely innocent man who couldn't help his looks.

Now people, did it pay? I'm sure it did. Good strong lasting lessons were being learned all day. Not the same for each, to be sure. No doubt to many of us the lessons were deeper and more lasting than they would have been, had the weather been auspicious.

It was a great disappointment to all when we had hoped for a glimpse, at least, of the world at our feet, from the summit, to be so enveloped by a cloud that we could only see each other indistinctly. But not one word of complaint was heard.

We are all going again. Come and join us.

I am persuaded that for pure refreshing, invigorating recreation which will strengthen our physical, mental and spiritual natures, nothing can surpass a mountain climb.

Moosilauke! Mossilauke!
Sis! Boom! Bah!
Newbury to Moosilauke!
Rah! Rah! Rah!

Appendix A

Eddy, Oklahoma
Jan. 24, 1907

Editor, United Opinion,

Oklahoma certainly has some interesting features, especially for a Yankee. I took a drive this morning of six miles across a flat country from Nardin, Oklahoma, to this town. No hills here to obstruct the views. The farms are all of 160 acres each, one quarter of a square mile, and the farmers have had such good crops the past year that [railroad] cars cannot be procured to take away the produce. Great heaps of corn may be seen being spoiled by the weather because cover has not been provided. The soil is rich and black and no fertilizer is needed. Great fields, green with winter wheat, are seen everywhere.

I found my train was two hours late, so I strolled over to the little town and found a shack with "Lunch Room" printed on the side, and as it was nearly noon, I went in. A good natured middle-aged woman was in attendance, and our interview ran thus:

Could I get a lunch here, please?
What do you want?
Well, have you any sandwiches?
I haint got any 'othem. Got some pie, though.
Have you any coffee?
Haint got any hot. Make ye some, though.
No, I don't think I will have time. I'll take a piece of pie and some cookies and a banana, please.

So while I ate, we talked and watched through the window for the train, which could be seen a long ways before it reached the station. I said: "This is one of the new towns that has sprung up within a few years."

"That's what it is. Had to build it all over again a second time, too."

"Why," I said, "How's that?"

"Cyclone."

"Oh, I see. Did it damage your property?"

"Damage it! Do you see that hotel over yonder?" I saw the oblong wooden building she indicated. "Well, we own that, and it was blown clean over to the railroad track (about ten rods) and tipped up on end, and it cost us a hundred and fifty dollars to put it back. We were goin' to build another story on it, but we got scared and put it on the end. You see it's longer than 'tis wide."

"Were you in it?" I asked.

"Come mighty near bein' in it. Just had time to get into the cellar. I got the money and my watch and Bill's and shut all the doors in the house and fastened 'em, and ran out, but the men had to pull me into the cellar…I couldn't stand…and I wasn't more than in when off she went right over our heads." "Why," she said, "there was a couple of young fellows just put in a stock of over two thousand dollars worth of goods in a new store and the whole store, goods and all, was all blown away, even to the foundations."

She saw my ignorance of those things and said, "I guess you're a stranger here, ain't ye?" I said, "Yes, I'm from the east."

"So'm I" she said, "I'm from Illanois."

I said, "I'm from Vermont."

I don't know whether she knew where Vermont was or not. She didn't seem much impressed.

I asked my driver the other day, with whom I was riding, if he knew where Vermont was, and he said "No"; he thought it was somewhere in the east, but he had never been east farther than Missouri.

I said, [continuing the conversation with the lunch counter lady] "Does the village dig a cyclone cellar to use in case of a storm?"

"The village! Every family has one. We haint had time to dig one yit, but we are goin' to, just as soon as we git to it."

I said, "Maybe you will never have another cyclone."

"Maybe not, but if we don't, it will be a handy thing to put fruit it. We've had some mighty high water here lately," she continued. "They had to run two heavy coal cars on to the railroad bridge down here to keep it from washing away." Quite a scheme, I thought.

The little school houses (*sic*) here and there look neat and trim, not unlike some of ours in Vermont, but I miss the flagpole. Perhaps after Oklahoma has been a state a while, she will adopt this excellent custom which will develop patriotism in the children.

The only mountains to be seen here are the mountain of wheat straw which really resemble mountain peaks when on the horizon. They tell me it is the custom to burn the straw as soon as it is threshed, but it seems it isn't always done.

I have seen only three Indians as yet: one boy and a real brave with his long braids wound with green ribbon and tucked down his coat collar. He didn't look romantic a bit, with a wide brimmed slouch hat, pulled down to his ears, a coat with the sleeves [too] long, and pants that were too small. I think he would have made a much better appearance with a bunch of feathers on his head and a blanket around him. The other one was a boy or young brave, with his braids worn in full view over his shoulders. I struck up an acquaintance with him on the train. His name was "Oscar Brave Bear." He said Brave Bear was his father's name, and seemed quite proud of it. He belong[s] to the Cheyenne tribe and had been to the Crow reservation in Minnesota to visit some friends, had been gone two months and was just getting home. He owns the government allowance of land, 160 acres, and he and his father and mother and grandmother live together. He said he got three hundred dollars from his wheat crop last year. He had been to school, studied all the common branches and gone as high as the seventh grade. He was quite interested in my camera and went out on the station platform and let me take his picture. I've always heard the Indians were stolid and uncommunicative as a race, but Oscar Brave Bear was very sociable to me.

I have seen just one Indian wigwam beside the railroad track, with a young Indian girl in a bright red shawl near by.

Well, I presume people make more money here than they do in old Vermont, but how anybody can stand it to stay in such a mixture of society I can't see. Give me Vermont hills for a country and native New Englanders for neighbors.

Yours truly,
C.R. Taggart

Jackson, Mississippi
Jan. 23, 1908

United Opinion Readers:

We have been having delightful weather for the past week. Windows open, birds singing, almost too warm to walk very fast without becoming heated.

This is the third State capitol I have visited within a week. Passed through Atlanta, Ga., just a week ago today, but did not have time to go to the state house [*sic*].

Appendix A

Last Saturday morning, I visited the old capitol building at Montgomery, Ala., and stood on the spot in the marble portico where Jef. Davis took his oath as president of the southern confederacy. The spot is marked by a brass star placed by the Daughters of the Confederacy, which seems to pervade this country. It seems to me that it would be better forgotten. There is a magnificent monument erected to the memory of the Confederate soldiers and sailors, with beautiful tributes in verse chiseled on the sides, near the Capitol, the cornerstone of which, according to the inscription, was laid by Jef. Davis [on] April 29th, 1886.

An old confederate soldier in a gray uniform showed me around. He was a little the worse for liquor, but discoursed quite freely, told several anecdotes of how he had given all the water in his canteen to wounded Yankees after battles, etc. He was quite interested to hear of my Yankee relatives who fought against him. About every battle I mentioned, he was there. Wilderness, was with Stonewall Jackson until he was shot. Was with Lee at Appomattox Court House, Bull Run, and I don't know how many more. About every old man here in the south you may count on as having been in the war, for they went almost to a man. Around the capitol building are trees brought from nearly all the battlefields and transplanted.

Today I spent an hour or two in the Legislature here in Jackson, and heard some very interesting speeches. The principal subject of discussion in the House seemed to be the sending of a committee to investigate matters at the four state colleges, and the difference of opinion was whether the committee should consist of three or eleven members. They finally decided that the state could afford to send eleven. One bill was read which caused a good deal of amusement, viz: To provide for a fixed marriage fee, not to be less than five dollars, nor more than a hundred and fifty. The House just shouted when it was read. I believe there was a provision that if the marrying parties were unable to pay, that the county or state should foot the bill. I missed the committee to which it was referred.

The Standard Oil Company must give up all hope of monopoly in Mississippi, if the bill and amendments go through which were under discussion in the Senate. They were dead in earnest amending old laws and making new ones to cover all possible infringements of the rights of the people concerning great corporations.

The next capital city I will visit will be Little Rock, Ark., but I only pass through with no time to see the state house, unless it may be seen from the train. Oklahoma City next Monday night, then into Texas for two weeks.

The millennium has begun in the South sure, as far as the liquor business is concerned. It did me good to see the saloons in Atlanta so dark and desolate. No whiskey in sight, except the dingy signs painted on the windows. People here say Mississippi will go dry very shortly. Our northern states should feel ashamed not to have had the honor of leading off, but let us follow suit immediately.

Wish I was home working on my woodpile, as Jack Harris suggests.

Very truly,
C.R. Taggart

Down in the Cotton Fields
Newton, Mississippi
October 15, 1913

Greetings from the south to readers of the Groton Times:

They tell us that October and November are beautiful months to travel in the south. I never was so hot in my life as I was the first week in October. It is much better now. Of course, if I had been dressed for summer, it would have been better.

This is the beginning of the cotton picking and ginning. In every town, we hear the pulling of the cotton gin, and the cotton pickers stand waist deep in the cotton field and watch the train go by.

Cotton is selling for about 14c. per pound. At the gin, the seeds are removed and the cotton bound into bales of 500 pounds each. A good field will yield a bale to the acre. The average price for picking is 50c. per hundred pounds, but late in the season, or when the price is small, or when the cotton has been picked over once, the price per hundred goes up for picking. One picks about three or four hundred pounds per day if he picks and [doesn't] watch the train all the time. The seeds are sold for about eight or ten dollars per ton.

The boll [weevil] is doing great damage to the cotton crop, so much so that some communities are seriously contemplating raising some other crop instead.

These Mississippi towns are built, many of them, in the form of a square (that is, the business section), with the court house [*sic*] in the center.

At Houston, Miss., they told us of a negro who was burned in Court House Square and later was proved innocent, but too late.

Appendix A

At Dora, Alabama, I found three traveling salesmen sitting on the porch of the hotel, busily engaged in discussing religion. When I arrived, they were in the profound depths of "Predestination" and "Man's free will." Imagine it in Groton, or Newbury!

The polite conversation of some of these lanky, round-shouldered, slouch-hatted Mississippians is noticeable. I heard two in the station today. One said, "Howdy, Sam. How's yo papa and mama?" "Mighty fine, thank you, Jim. How are you all?"

Committees here are enthusiastic over their lecture courses. I have been met at the train at nearly every new town by one, and sometimes two of the committee. The people are generally cordial and appreciative, and under these conditions, they get the very best work from their talent.

I trust that none of the talent that comes to our Vermont towns, which have lecture courses, will be left to find their way to a hotel as best they can, and inquire the way to the hall or church. It is a lonesome life, going about among strangers for months at a time, and we look forward to meeting pleasant friends in the towns where we stop, and when we alight from the train and see only a gaping crowd, and tug our own luggage to a hotel, and find possibly one of the kind where we don't feel like even unpacking our grip—dirty wash bowl, not even a nail to hang a hat, dim, smoky lamp, bad food, and perhaps the committee, after we have hunted him up, says, "Just go ahead when you get ready. We don't introduce people here"; and where the audience gets up and departs with no words of cheer; we shake off the dust of our feet in such places and feel like going out of the business. But it is not often so bad as this.

Wish I could see the beautiful Vermont forests with their gay autumn robes.

Not a word about Harry Thaw in the papers here just now, but plenty about the race between Underwood and Hobson in Alabama politics.

I will begin work in Michigan, and the states of the middle west next Tuesday.

Sincerely,
C.R. Taggart

Appendix A

Princeton, MN
July 19, 1918

Dear Opinion Readers,

I have just received my OPINION and read it with interest as usual. I am traveling from place to place on the Midland Chautauqua Circuit with ex-Warden [James C.] Sanders, formerly of the Fort Madison, Iowa State Penitentiary. He lectures on the reforms he instituted there. His son, Roger, a boy fifteen years old, also travels with us, and he operates the U.S. Government War Pictures as part of the evening program. And we all travel together in a FORD. I sit on the back seat with the picture machine, film box, and numerous suitcases and traveling bags piled around me to keep me in place. It is delightful skimming along over these fine graveled roads between the oat, wheat, barley, corn and flax fields of Minnesota. Hundreds of little gophers about the size of a chipmunk scamper across the road in front of the car. They say they are a great pest to the growing grain. They dig in and eat the roots.

I work twice a day a prelude for Warden Sanders at three and my regular program at eight-thirty.

In some towns in this state, there are a good many pro-Germans, but they keep their heads down and the patriotic utterances from the Chautauqua platform are usually well applauded.

I see you had a grand celebration in Bradford on the Fourth of July. One of the right sort for the times.

My work this summer is all in Iowa, Minnesota and Wisconsin. Community sings are getting common everywhere here in the West. Let's get 'em a going in Vermont. Let us get all the cornets, fiddles and everything anybody can play a tune on into action and plan for one evening in a week, in the largest hall in town, and sing the good old songs and good new ones. All together! Everybody! According to the papers to-day, we will all **want** to sing songs of victory before long, and we might as well get tuned up.

I would like to see Old Newbury start into this with both sleeves rolled up.

[I] expect to be home and ready to fill local Red Cross dates after August 20.

Cordially,
C.R. Taggart

Appendix A

On train in Michigan
Feb. 26, 1919

Dear Opinion Readers,

I am interested just at this time in the stories of the forest fires that swept northeastern Michigan in 1908. The hotel keeper at Oscoda, Mich., told me enough of the awfulness of it to awaken my interest and now, as my train is passing through the very region where the worst fires occurred, I took pains to make a few inquiries. The track runs through what was once the Forest Primeval—stumps, underbrush, and thousands of charred tree trunks. I asked the brakeman some questions, and as he was working on this road at the time of the fire, he gave me some interesting details. I saw in the R.R. station at Oscoda a sign, warning the public to be careful about cigar and cigarette stumps and burned matches, and campfires, etc., and as a special warning, the placard read "Remember Metz and Au Sable." There were whole towns that were wiped out by the fires. Our train just passed thro' Metz a few moments ago. When the people of Metz saw the fire approaching, they ran, panic-stricken, from their homes and a freight train came along just then, and many climbed aboard into a steel coal car, and the engineer tried to rush the train away, but at a small town near Metz, the smoke was so dense he could not see that the fire had twisted the rails and the train was wrecked, and the train crew and all aboard were burned to death. Seventeen in all.

The homeless were destitute, and relief trains brought them food, and lumber for shacks, for shelter, until they could build themselves houses. Enough lumber to build a shack 16 x 20 feet was furnished to each family. The brakeman tells me he brought bags of sandwiches, and the people actually fought for them.

In many places in the forest, where they had been lumbering, piles of brush were left and these made an exceedingly hot fire. I think we read in a general way of these fires at the time, but they were so far away we did not fully realize the awfulness of them.

Ever since I read the old fourth reader in school, the story of "Me's Race for Life," and saw the picture of the family piled in the farm wagon, huddled together with the farmer lashing the wild horses to a run, with the flames roaring behind them, I have had a horror of forest fires. The vast extent of forest land is being cleared up so rapidly, such stories will be mere recollections before many years.

The town of Oscoda was all burned but 49 houses, on July 11, 1911. A hundred and fifty people were assembled on a dock between the burning town and the lake and only the timely arrival of a lumber boat, which took the people off, saved them from either drowning or burning.

What a hell on earth they have had over between Toledo and Detroit, with the Rum Runners defying the law openly, carrying thousands of quarts of whiskey from Ohio to Michigan, but the voice of the people of the Country, the sane, sober, majority, has spoken, saying the whole rum business has proved itself a nuisance, and must stop.

Last night, I slept in Petosky, where I could hear the waves of Lake Michigan splashing the shore, and to-night I will sleep at Alpena, within a stone's throw of Lake Huron.

Bradford people are doubtless proud of the fact that one of her former townsmen is now Governor of this big state. He has been a busy man lately with the Booze war, and the investigations of the Industrial Schools for girls at Adrian, but he seems to measure up to the task as a Vermonter would be expected to do.

I expect to be home by the middle of March.

The "Flu" [Spanish influenza] is still present in Northern Michigan. Just had two dates cancelled on account of it.

Cordially,
C.R.Taggart

Appendix B

SELECTED POEMS OF CHARLES ROSS TAGGART

Oklahoma

(Written in Oklahoma City on January 27, 1907)

Ye who love our glorious country,
Love its graceful, winding rivers,
Love its high and rugged mountains,
Love its broad and waving prairies,
Listen to my song of travel,
From the fruitful western prairies,
From the new state of our Union,
From the state of Oklahoma.

Should you ask me of the people
That inhabit this new country,
Of their manners and their customs,
Of their various occupations,
I should answer, I should tell you
All the people here are strangers,
From some other state or country,
Wandered here for various reasons.
Some for love of pure adventure,
More to make a rapid fortune
From the wonderful resources

Of this new and growing country.
Some are farmers, some are merchants,
Others, ranchmen, cattle buyers.

Many are the occupations
Of the people of this country,
Of this state of Oklahoma.
Hearty words of welcome issue
From their lips to greet the stranger;
Kindly eyes with friendly glances
Look from under wide sombreros;
Strong and warm the hand of greeting
Of these pioneers of fortune.
All are brothers, friends and neighbors
On these broad and fertile prairies
Of the new state of our Union,
Of the state of Oklahoma.

This was once the red man's country;
All his right and title to it
Given him by the Great Spirit
Gitche Manito, the mighty.
But the red man's sun is setting;
All the wilderness and the romance
Of the past are now departed,
And the memory of it only
Lives in poem and in story.

Should you ask me of the climate
Of this state of Oklahoma
I should answer, I should tell you,
Warm and fresh have been the breezes
Wafted to me o'er the prairies;
Warm and sunny shone the heavens
Smiling upon all the landscape.
But they tell me mighty windstorms
Come with terrible destruction
And the west wind, Mudjekeewis,
Rushing eastward o'er the mountains,

Blows upon them with his nostrils,
Blows upon the waving cornfields,
Making them bow low in terror
At the fury of his vengeance.

Yes, the prairies have their beauties
In their broad and waving meadows,
In the grandeur of the outlook,
In the width of the horizon,
In the broad expanse of heavens.
But I love the mountains better,
Love their high and gusty summits,
Love the shadow of the forest.

Love the wind among the branches
And the rain shower and the snow storm,
And the rushing of the rivers
Through their palisades of pine trees.
And the thunder in the mountains,
Whose innumerable echoes
Flap like eagles in their eyries,
For my home is in the highlands,
In the highlands of New England,
In the kingdom of the North Wind
In the regions of the morning.

Ye who love our glorious nation,
Love her graceful, winding rivers,
Love her wooded hills and mountains,
Love her broad and waving prairies,
Greet our distant friends and brothers
In the kingdom of the West Wind,
Toward the portals of the sunset.
Let the people of New England
In the Northlands and the mountains,
From the Appalachian Mountains,
From the shores of the Atlantic,
Greet our western friends and brothers,
Greet them, speaking words on this wise.

Appendix B

We rejoice to have you with us,
Youngest of Columbia's daughters.
One more star has now been added
To the banner of our nation.
We are brothers, friends and neighbors.
Welcome! Welcome! Oklahoma.

Vermont Song
(to the tune of "A Fine Old English Gentleman")

I'll sing you an old ballad
About a grand old state
Whose size upon the map is small,
Tho' really she is great.
As first born of the nation
In seventeen ninety-one.
A new star shone upon our flag
And her history was begun.
We love our own, our native land,
The Old Green Mountain State.

When in her early history
She needed men to fight,
They were not wanting, but arose
And bared their arms of might.
They bade defiance to the foe
Who sought to bind us down,
And said, "Vermont yields never
To the mandates of the Crown."
The bold Green Mountain Boys were they,
The sons of old Vermont.

Young Ethan Allen when a boy
Did never fear the dark;
At Bennington, the Hessians feared
The name of General Stark.

Appendix B

These men and others like them,
In those rugged days of old,
Won their country's praise and honor
By their deeds of valor bold.
They're every one Green Mountain Boys,
The sons of old Vermont.

The Hero of Manila Bay
Knew what he was about;
At the noble deed of Dewey there,
The world sent up a shout.
The Oregon and Captain Clark
Received the honor due,
From people and from president,
And all the nations, too.
They're every one Green Mountain Boys
The sons of old Vermont.

Our state is rich in all the wealth
That nature has to give,
The boys and girls of old Vermont
Know what it is to live.
Our pumpkin pies are genuine,
Our honey is made by bees,
Our maple sugar is made from sap
That comes from maple trees.
We love the hills and valleys
In the old Green Mountain State.

Just one more word about our state,
I wish to say to you:
We're just *one* star upon the flag
In all the field of blue.
In Uncle Sam's Inheritance
Of states, both great and small,
The same flag floats above us
That floats above them all—
The stars and stripes forever
For the old Green Mountain State.

Appendix B

Hiawatha Visits the Chautauqua

"Ye whose hearts are fresh and simple,
Who have faith in God and Nature,
Who believe that in all ages
Every human heart is human."
Come with me, and let us follow
Hiawatha, as he journeys
In the kingdom of the prairies,
In the land of the Chautauquas.

Many moons have come and vanished
Since the time of his departure
In the glory of the sunset
To the regions of the West Wind,
When the Black Robe chief, the Pale Face,
Landed on the sandy margin
Of the shores of Gitche Gumee
By the shining Big-Sea-Water.

Now he comes again amoung us,
Comes to "stop, and look, and listen,"
All intent to catch the spirit
Of this wondrous race of people.

Tossed and streamed his raven tresses,
As he strode forth o'er the prairies
With his moccasins enchanted.
All the land was strangely altered;
Gone were all the waving forests,
And instead were Pale Face dwellings;
Houses, windmills, towns and cities.
But at length he spied a wigwam,
Large and round, and filled with people
In a lovely grove of pine trees.

Appendix B

How his heart did leap within him,
As he neared the great Chautauqua!
Straight he donned his cloak of magic,
Took a seat among the people,
Listened to the words of wisdom,
Wondered greatly as he listened.
Then he saw a great magician
Fill the multitude with wonder
By his marv'lous transformations—
Then he heard the sweetest music
Ever tho't of, or imagined.
Here he stayed, enchanted, spellbound,
Till the program was completed
And the multitude departed.

With his moccasins, enchanted,
Many days and weeks he journeyed
In the land of the Chautauquas,
Entering the crowded wigwams,
Sitting silently among them
Hidden in his cloak of magic.

Should you ask me, Why this journey?
I will let him give the answer.

"I will tell you, O, my brothers,
Why I came again among you.

"From the regions of the Sunset
I have come to learn the secret
Of your ever-growing nation;
Come to see why all your customs
Make such clean and happy people
All at peace with one another.

"With my moccasins, enchanted,
I have roamed o'er all your country,
Trod your valleys, climbed your mountains,
Seen your towns, and seen your cities.

Appendix B

Yet the answer to my questions
I have found upon the prairies,
In the land of the Chautauquas.

"In the pleasant days of summer,
There the people all assemble,
All the young men and the old men,
All the wives and young papooses,
All the young and blushing maidens,
There in pleasant woodsy places,
Underneath the mighty wigwams,
And with gently blowing breezes
Playing in and out among them.
Hear and see the things that please them;
Making them forget their sorrows.
And their hearts are cheered and brightened
As their merry shouts of laughter
Greet the marv'lous story-tellers;
As they see the great magicians
Do their wondrous feats of magic.
And they sit in silent rapture
While the witching strains of music
Fill their hearts with love and longing.

"There they hear the famous speakers—
'Lecturers,' the people call them—
Teachers, leaders of the people,
Mighty chiefs, and priests, and sachems,
Who, with cunning words of wisdom,
Lead the people upward, outward;
Show them better plans for farming,
How to make more sav'ry dishes;
Teach them many hidden secrets
Gathered from the distant kingdoms.
There they learn of truth and beauty,
And they clap their hands together
In their buoyancy of spirit
And their gratitude and pleasure,
That for merely gold and silver,

Appendix B

That for only beads and wampum
Given to the 'wampum-keepers'
In the kingdom of the Bureaus,
They may sit beneath the wigwams
And enjoy these things that please them,
And that make their journey brighter
Toward the Islands of the Blessed,
Toward the kingdom of Ponemah,
Toward the land of the Hereafter."

With these words, my Hiawatha
"Turned, and waved his hand at parting,
Launched his birch canoe for sailing,
Shoved it forth into the water;
And with speed it darted forward
Toward the kingdom of the Home-wind
Toward the regions of the sunset."

Appendix C

SELECTED "OLD COUNTRY FIDDLER" MONOLOGUES OF CHARLES ROSS TAGGART

(transcribed by Adam R. Boyce)

The Old Country Fiddler and the Bandit

I've been a'reading in the papers lately a good deal about the new systems of dealing with crime. From all I've heered, they used to hang folks and chop their heads off and burn 'em alive when they didn't go straight. But now they put 'em in a nice warm jail in a nice warm room, give 'em a good bed and plenty ta eat, and if they're bad enough, the women bring in flowers and sing to 'em, and after a good long trial, when they get their pictures and names in the papers and have a chance to attend court and set in a reserved seat for a good many performances, then they go to a shoe factory and work 'till the governor pardons 'em out, and then somebody writes a book about 'em and sells it on the train for 25 cents. Consequently, 'tain't quite so risky to break the law as it used to be, and seeing the details of interesting misdemeanors that I pulled out some nights in the newspapers, 'tain't no wonder that boys like to try the schemes they read about, and if they do get ketched, they don't worry much about it, for they know that when they get out, they'll always have something to look back to and brag about.

Appendix C

Well, after thinking this thing over one day, I surprised Moriah by asking her if she could make me a black mask. After she recovered from the shock, I says, "I'm going inta the bandit business," I says. "I've been to a highly moral picture show, passed by the National Board of Censors, and I see a fella there that held up stage coaches in a nice, gentlemanly way, and only took money from rich scalawags who didn't need it, and was nice and polite to women folks and took off his hat to gals, and, say, Moriah," says I, "he was loved and respected by the audience a pesky site more than the sheriff that ketched him. So," I says, "I've discovered that a long way back when we was young, keeping the law was considered most respectable. Nowadays, the law breakers are the heroes, so I'm going to get out that old Colt revolver up in the attic and divide up the cash in this community a little more evenly."

"Now," says Moriah, "You looka here! I shan't have you go to murdering folks."

"Oh," I says, "I ain't a'goin' ta shoot nobody. You couldn't make that old weapon go off if you should try," I says. "The high-class bandits don't shoot nobody—they just scare 'em." I says, "There's some folks in this town I think t'would do 'em good to be held up. It might lead 'em to consider their latter end and meditate on the brevity of life some." I says, "Perhaps I could do a lot of good in the community this way." But Moriah, she says, "Well, I shan't listen a minute to no such plan."

So, as I didn't want ta start a rout, I had to give it up, but BY JIMMINY CRICKETS! I don't see why t'would be any worse for some of them rich dudes to be relieved of some of their superfluous cash at the point of a pistol that wouldn't shoot than for good honest folks to be held up by some combination of trusts. The only difference I can see is that in the case of the trusts, we call it business, and with the bandit, we call it crime. We had a lecturer over at the hall one day who said everybody meant well, and that if everybody had a house and a garden and a lawnmower and a Ford and a pianer, and pretty pictures on the wall, and didn't have to work but six hours a day, they would all be good and happy and go to church and ta heaven when they died, and there wouldn't be no criminals, but BY JINKS! I believe there's a whole lot of folks that find it more interesting and exciting to do wrong than to do right, 'specially when the penalty don't scare 'em none. I guess it's a good deal as Mark Twain said, "Be good, and you'll be lonesome."

Well, seeing Moriah object so strong to the hold-up business, I guess I'll have to keep on tapping shoes for a living.

I guess I'll have to play the Rogue's March after that…

[plays "Rogue's March" on fiddle]

Appendix C

The Old Country Fiddler and the Book Agent

One day last spring, I was a'settin' on my porch, a fiddlin' away, when I see a fella that I took to be a book agent coming up the path, with a four-pound volume of literature under his arm. He was a kind of a spindling, sickly looking chap, with a green hat pulled clean down to the tops of his ears and a suit of store clothes on. He didn't look as if he had gumption enough to sell peanuts to a boy, but he stepped up as pert as a rooster and said, ah, "Good Morning, Reuben! I've got a book here on raising calves I thought you'd like to look at."

"Well," I says, "if you've got a book on raising calves, you better make a present of it to your parents. I think 'twould be profitable reading for 'em"… heh, heh…

But lands sakes, 'twarn't no use—HE couldn't *see* the pint!

The name of his book was *Carter's Complete and Comprehensive Compendium of Indispensable Information*. It did seem to have a lot in it. Besides the treatise on raising calves, it told you what to do when you loose your jackknife, and how many men taking hold of hands 'twould take to reach around the Atlantic Ocean, what to do first after you get drownded, and how high all the mountains in the world would be piled up on top of one another, and ah, what to do when the whiffletree breaks and how to run a sewing machine, how many Democrats there are in Mississippi and how many Republicans in Vermont and ah, most anything anybody wanted to know…heh, heh.

Well, I didn't seem to hanker for all that information jest that minute, so I sent him over to the minister. Moriah, she was over to the Widda Salby's when he called on her, and when the widda found his name was Bunker, she asked him if he was any relation to old cross-eyed Pete Bunker, used to live over on Goose Medder. He said he warn't, but the widda entertained him for hours with the history of the whole Bunker family, heh, heh, so the fella couldn't get in a word edgewise about his book. But when the widda found the book had a brand-new receipt for making boiled cider applesass, she said she'd take it, if he'd take his pay in board. Well, he agreed, so she put him to sleep in the room where her first husband hung himself, and related all the circumstances to him, and the fella got so scared in the night that he jumped out the window, walked clear to Slocum Junction, and ain't been heard from since. The only other book he sold as I heard was to Ab Tolliver, and Ab told him he'd take the book if he took his pay in potatoes. Fella said he would—price of the book was four dollars, so Ab give him two bushels of potatoes at two dollars a bushel…heh, heh…and the fella borrowed a wheelbarrow and waddle-wheeled them two miles down to Sile Haskins's store and offered to sell them to Sile. Well, Sile said that potatoes was worth JUUUUST EXACTLY thirty cents a bushel, so the fella got mad and went off and left 'em a'settin' on the store steps and they're there yet, as far as I know.

I reckon the Pineville folks didn't really want quite such much promiscus information all in one dose. Fact is, I didn't myself.

[fiddles]

The Old Country Fiddler at the Wedding

Hey, that Victrola thar'n come pretty near getting me into about the worst scrape I was ever in. You see, it was the time of Jenny Sullivan's wedding. She and Dick Mastin been going together for nigh onto four years, and so they thought 'twas about time to get hitched up. Dick, he wanted to have a swell wedding in the meetinghouse, but Jenny said no—she was going to be married to home. Well, I didn't blame her a mite, but there was just one objection to being married to home—they had no pianer nor organ in the house, and Jenny, she wanted a wedding march played. She wanted to march around awhile before she was married, I suppose. So she come over to see if I'd bring my fiddle over and play the wedding march for 'em. Lands sakes, I'd do anything for Jenny—knowed her ever since she was a baby, so I went over.

I found Jenny and Dick and the minister, and that was all! I says, eh, "Ain't you gonna have nobody else to the wedding?" Oh, they said, this waren't the wedding, this was just a re-hearsal to try over the ceremony to see how the proceedings was going to operate the next day. You see, they'd invited a whole houseful of folks and they was a'wonderin' where they was going to have room to march.

Well, they finally decided they'd start in the spare room and march around through the kitchen, and the buttery, and wind up in the parlor and be married under the looking glass. They put me up in the sink in the buttery, so I'd be out of the way. And when they got ALL ready, I started out "Marching Through Georgia," but they come a'running in, said that weren't the tune. They said there was a special piece just for weddings. WELL, I thought I was up the stump there for a minute, but all of a sudden I happened to think of my talking machine and I says, "Say, I'll bring over my Victrola, and we'll let that do the playing." And I asked the Elder if he supposed they had a record of that wedding march, and he said he thought probably they DID, so I telephoned down to the Junction and found out they had one, and the hardware man said he'd send it right up.

Well, it didn't get there in time for NO rehearsal, but it come JEST in time for the wedding. That postmaster's boy come a'lugging it over under his arm. Like a fool, I forgot my glasses, but I managed to get the wrappers off and the needle put in and was all ready to set it a'whirling. Pretty soon, the elder come, tapped me on the shoulder and said they was ALL ready, so I started it up.

BUT! Of all the tunes for a wedding march, I never heered the beat! Started out with a rattling good jig and pretty soon a chorus bust loose with: *[to the playing of "Irish Washerwoman" in the key of C]*

Did you ever walk into an Irishman's shanty
Where people, potatoes and cabbage are plenty,
A breeze'll get through the tables and mash
From the door to the shanty from under the latch

WELL, there were some surprised folks around there now, you bet, but they got started, so they went ahead. Dick, he yanked Jenny 'round through the buttery so fast, he knocked the tea kettle off the stove and they got into the parlor 'fore the Elder found his place and, well, after it 'twas all over, Elder Belker come in and said he *thought that tune* was a *little might rapid* for a wedding march. Well, I told him I thought it twas myself.

Just about that time, that postmaster's boy come a luggin' another bundle. You see, they sent up two records: one for Ab Toliver and one for me, and that boy got 'em mixed up. WELL, I give that boy a piece of my mind, now I tell ye. Now the right one went like this:

[plays wedding march recessional]

'Course, Jenny was awfully disappointed not to have the right one—you know how gals feel about such things—but Dick said the first one was the best—heh heh. He said he didn't want to poke along all day—he wanted to get in there and have it over with!

Oh well, I got out of it better than I was afraid I should.

Appendix C

The Old Soldier's Vision

I was sittin' one day by my windder, a'watchin' a big parade,
With banners and flags a'flyin' and people of every grade,
When I heered a band a'comin', a'playin' a tune I knowed,
And I took my cane and started to meet 'em on the road;
Children were out by the hundreds, holding their Ma's by the hand
And everybody was harkin' to hear that wonderful band;
It came on nearer and nearer, the drum kept sounding the beat,
And the band kept on a'marchin' and poundin' the ground with its feet.

[chords on fiddle]

And all of a sudden they started and played an old time tune
That carried me back to the "Muster" and the old June training in June;
'Twas "On the Road to Boston," and it thrilled me through and through,
And I kept the step right with 'em, the same as I used to do.

[Plays "On The Road to Boston" in G]

When I heered that old "Road to Boston," I could see them old grounds again,
For I was a soldier as good as the rest, I didn't hobble then;
I could see my comrades there with me, I could feel their shoulders touch mine,
And the ground, it shook as it used ta, with the tramp of the long blue line;
I could hear the rattle of my skin as I shouted "SHOULDER ARMS"
And the weapons all blanched in the sunlight agin;
The vision was full of its charm, for I was a Captain in them days,
And commanded a hundred men—I could see 'em right there before me,
Looking jest as they all did then.

But the band has stopped the playin' of that grand old muster tune,
And the vision is growing dimmer, and all will be faded soon;
And when I come to my senses, I was standing there on the ground,
My cane was over my shoulder, and my hair was a'flyin' around;
"Three cheers for the band," I shouted, then the crowd took it up with a will,
"You can't beat the old Road to Boston," I said; methinks I can hear it still.
The procession kept on a'movin', the drum kept sounding the beat,
And the band kept on a'marchin' and pounding the ground with its feet;

Appendix C

And I hobbled back to my window agin', and sank down inta my chair,
To dream once more of the days of yore which the old tune brought back to me there.

[Plays "On The Road to Boston"]

BIBLIOGRAPHY

Blaisdell, Katharine. "Community Life: A Traveling Entertainer From Newbury." Chap. 2 in *Over the River and Through the Years*. Book 6, pp.117–26. North Haverhill, NH: printed by the Courier Printing Company (self-published by Katharine Blaisdell), 1984.

Greer, Lois Goodwin. "The Man from Vermont." *The Vermonter* 32, no. 6 (1927), 83–87.

Northfield Mount Hermon archives; Student Files; Taggart, Charles Ross #813MH: 1889 application information, letters and final post card Taggart wrote to the school in 1953.

Redpath Chautauqua Bureau Collection, University of Iowa Libraries, Iowa City, Iowa, Series 1—Talent; Taggart, Charles Ross, MsC 150, boxes 318–19: Letters between Charles Ross Taggart and the Redpath Bureau; States Program box 409 (Vermont): copy of Montpelier Chautauqua brochure, 1927.

Taggart, Charles Ross. Article to *Vermont Life* magazine, which was never published, circa 1946, and other letters and poems, which originally appeared in *The United Opinion*, *The Groton Times*, *The Barre Daily Times*, and *The Lyceum Magazine*, courtesy of the Newbury, Vermont Historical Society.

———. Letter to his mother, Emily (Divoll) Taggart, written while at Mount Hermon, dated January 16, 1890, courtesy of the Topsham (Vermont) Historical Society.

INDEX

I

J

K

L

M

R

S

T

U

V

W

Index

ABOUT THE AUTHOR

Adam Boyce, 2010. *Julie Ireland Photography.*

Adam Boyce, whose family has called Vermont home since the 1760s, has been a lifelong student of history. He grew up on a farm in Williamstown, which his great-grandfather purchased in 1896 and was the same place where his father and grandfather were also raised.

Much like Charles Ross Taggart, Adam has had a myriad of vocations and interests, including farm worker and school janitor. He held a number of elected positions in his former hometown of Williamstown, including town moderator.

Beginning in 1991, he took fiddle lessons from nationally recognized Yankee fiddler Harold Luce of Chelsea and got immersed in learning about the local traditional dance and music history of central Vermont, including fiddling and calling simultaneously for square and contra dances. Adam was the 2000 Vermont division winner of the former Northeast Fiddlers' contest at Barre and has competed in nearly every New England state. He has become a recognized authority on all these

Author Adam Boyce portraying Charles Ross Taggart's "Old Country Fiddler," 2010. *Julie Ireland Photography.*

traditions and has been a partner on special projects with the Vermont Folklife Center in Middlebury.

In 2001, he started doing lectures for local nonprofit groups through the Speakers' Bureau of the Vermont Humanities Council, and in 2005, he was also added to the New Hampshire *Humanities to Go!* Adam's research about Charles Ross Taggart led him to venture into presenting living history portrayals, starting in 2010.

A composer of more than one hundred fiddle tunes, he is a juried artist with the Vermont Arts Council and has appeared in several central Vermont stage productions, including Lost Nation Theater in Montpelier and George Woodard's Ground Hog Opry out of Waterbury.

Adam and his wife, Mary-Anne, live in West Windsor, Vermont.

Visit us at
www.historypress.net

This title is also available as an e-book

www.ingramcontent.com/pod-product-compliance
Lightning Source LLC
LaVergne TN
LVHW010947100826
845153LV00002B/161

* 9 7 8 1 5 4 0 2 2 2 3 4 3 *